HOW TO SURVIVE
THE
MONEY CRASH

Ne
ho
fro   Doug Clark to you.

Each month, you'll learn
how new world, national
and local developments
in politics and
economics will affect you
and how to prepare for
them.

You'll learn new ways to:
- Protect yourself and
  your loved ones from
  coming economic
  chaos
- Protect your property
- Survive famine, civil
  unrest and all-out war
  . . . and more.

FREE BONUS

As a subscriber, you'll
receive a FREE copy of
Doug Clark's exciting
new book, **They Saw The
Second Coming,** an
explosive novel about the
end of the world.

SPECIAL DISCOUNT
OFFER

. . . see card inside
back cover.

HOW TO SURVIVE THE MONEY CRASH

Doug Clark

Harvest House Publishers
Irvine, California 92714

ABOUT THE AUTHOR

Doug Clark, host of "Amazing Prophecy" television program, has been specializing in the study of economics, political science and biblical prophecies for over 20 years. He has done graduate work at Holmes Theological Seminary and the University of Toronto, and has traveled extensively around the world.

Doug and his wife, Charlene, are currently involved in seminars on biblical prophecy and the alarming developments in the money markets. His books and newsletters combine a penetrating analysis of biblical prophecies with both financial and political forecasting, and are a helpful guide to thousands in an age of uncertainty.

Doug Clark's new best-seller, HOW TO SURVIVE THE MONEY CRASH, is a must for all readers.

HOW TO SURVIVE THE MONEY CRASH

Copyright ©1979 Harvest House Publishers
Irvine, California 92714
Library of Congress Catalog Card Number: 78-71426
ISBN 0-89081-188-1

Printed in the United States of America.

CONTENTS

INTRODUCTION

Frightening Questions About Your Financial Future

Read about your financial future in this book. Your future could be filled with depression, sadness, and terrible loss, or it could be filled with exciting success and marvelous financial assets, even to the point of making a fortune while others whom you know fall into bankruptcy.

We will ask and answer these questions:

WILL THERE BE A DEPRESSION IN AMERICA SOON?

WILL THE BANKS CRASH AND CLOSE AS THEY DID IN 1929?

WILL THE DOLLAR DIE COMPLETELY?

WHAT IS GOING TO HAPPEN TO GOLD AND SILVER?

IS THERE A REAL CONSPIRACY TO OVERTHROW THE DOLLAR?

WILL THE GOVERNMENT FALL?

IN THE USA ARE WE HEADED TOWARD THE EUROPEAN ONE-WORLD GOVERNMENT?

HOW CAN I SURVIVE ALL THIS AND COME OUT ON TOP?

Many other alarming questions will be asked and answered, all of them affecting you and your future in one way or another. Many of the facts you are already painfully aware of. For instance, you know the dollar is dying in purchasing power every week. But why is it dying? What will become of us unless this decline is stopped?

In the future, how will you live, where will you live, and how well off will you be when the dollar dies?

Many other authors are adding their severe warnings about the next five years, similar to what I am saying but from their own point of view. I trust that this accumulation of facts, together with the outlook presented through the prophecies of the Bible, will give you the best guidance for the future you want to enjoy despite the most startling circumstances you have ever lived under!

Recently, 135 finance ministers representing nations from all over the noncommunist world met with about the same number of World Bank governors and more than 3000 financial and economic experts in Washington, D.C., for the 33rd annual joint conference of the World Bank and the International Monetary Fund.

There was a somber, funeral air as they met, with many of the participants feeling that this could be the last meeting of its kind.

The reason for this extreme sadness was the sober fact that 11 European nations had already met and signed an agreement to virtually "dump the dollar" and form a totally European currency for the purpose of producing European monetary unity.

In spite of much pressure brought to bear on the 11 nations by the others who were fighting for the very existence of the U.S. dollar, the finance ministers held firm for the new monetary system to be set up in December of this year (1978).

European leaders such as West German Chancellor Helmut Schmidt and French President Valery Giscard d'Estaing (plus certain British leaders) all agree that "the moment has come to break away from Washington and the dying dollar." They believe that "unless we want a crash, we must pull ourselves free from the dollar noose. America's fiscal policies will pull us down to perdition."

The New Euro-currency, designated ECU, presents a profound and potentially fatal challenge to the dollar's position as the world's premier reserve and denominator currency.

A number of OPEC nations (oil-producing exporting countries) announced that they would drop the dollar and turn to the gold-backed ECU upon its entrance to the world's money markets.

This is not an idle threat by the Europeans. They have already set up the creation of the ECU, the timing of its introduction, and the institutional framework to circulate and support it. It is an act of self-defense against the dying dollar and the lack of its support by the U.S.

Supposedly before the end of 1978, Europe will adopt the ECU as its new currency, ending a quarter-century era during which the U.S. dollar reigned supreme as the reserve, denominator, and unquestioned fixed star of the world's fiscal firmament. ECU will become a "global currency" immediately, notes a British journalist specializing in economic affairs: "At first only large banknotes analogous to U.S. Treasury notes will be printed for use in interbank and intercorporate transactions. But eventually the ECU will serve as a genuine European currency, as readily acceptable in Portugal as in Ireland, and in due course also in nations outside the European Economic Community, which (will) learn to trust and use our central tender much as they have been using the dollar for decades."

ECU will probably make its appearance as a glamorous new world currency in January, 1979 or shortly thereafter, according to the best brains on the subject. Europe is now ready for it. The American dying dollar is the chief contributor to the necessity of it now.

As ECU arrives, so will the all-new EUROPEAN MONETARY FUND, which will soon take the place of the dying INTERNATIONAL MONETARY FUND, set up by the U.S. at the end of World War II to help ailing nations. This new "bank" in Europe will act against the IMF and will replace it, using ECU as the currency for international exchange. It will dump the dollar.

The EMF will by this time next year—or sooner—be functioning with ECU and with assets set initially at 50 billion ECUs ($64 billion), half in gold and half in hard currency. This great European challenge to the U.S. dollar's supremacy is now irrevocably launched, and will be further described in this book.

All of this has come about as a result of government-induced inflation here in the United States, which has contributed to the speedy demise of the dollar and to your bankruptcy and mine, unless we personally do something tangible about it **now**. In this book you will learn what is happening and how you can survive and come out on top in spite of the crash of the dollar.

Chapter

1

The Cancerous Dollar and Its Innocent Victims

The agonies of the dying dollar shock us every day. With the subtility of a slithering snake in the high grass, the federal-government-induced inflation is strangling the life out of your last dollar. As a snake entwines itself around a sleeping fisherman on the banks of a river and then suddenly squeezes him until it crushes the life out of him, so our dollar is being attacked, crushed, and destroyed every day by the gradual squeezing of the politically guided economic forces around us.

Your Dollar Is Dying Daily

We are going to determine why, what can be done about it, how you can survive it, and how you can come out on top financially.

Assuming the dollar was worth 100 cents at the time of Franklin Roosevelt's death in 1945, then in Truman's day it dropped in purchasing power 66.8 cents (5.3 percent inflation); Eisenhower, 59.7 cents (1.4 percent inflation); Kennedy, 57.7 cents (1.2 percent inflation); Johnson 50.0 cents (2.8 percent inflation); Nixon, 35.6 cents (6.3 percent inflation); Ford, 30.4 cents (6.7 percent inflation); and Carter, after one and a half years in office, 27 cents (10 percent current inflation rate). No wonder Americans have consumer jitters, with over 65 percent of the people believing that we are going to have a recession-depression right away!

Canadians are even worse off than Americans, since their dollar is slipping even faster than the United States currency.

But what is happening in American monetary circles is also happening in currencies in Europe, only not as flagrantly and fatally as it is here in the United States and Canada.

The fact that the dollar is dying is evident in the erosion of its purchasing power every week. The cost of living is rising astronomically while the value of the dollar is dropping shockingly.

Imported goods are rising in price for all Americans and we wonder why. Coffee, tea, automobiles, various foodstuffs—as a matter of fact, over 25 percent of the goods we use daily in our homes and businesses—are imported to us. The costs are going out of sight.

This year alone there has been a 23 percent increase in the price of food in the United States!

Imported television sets, radios, and similar components have risen in price sharply.

Unions are demanding higher and higher wage scales so employees can keep up the cost-of-living increases monthly.

Prices are on the rise on domestically produced products as well, so that manufacturers can keep up with the costs of living and being in business. Raw materials, many of which are imported, have reached all-time highs in costs for the manufacturers, resulting in inevitable price rises for manufactured goods.

Of the 54 kinds of imported raw materials used by the U.S., 38 come from the Indian Ocean countries, and more than 80 percent of America's tin and rubber requirements come from Southeast Asia. Every 13 minutes a tanker leaves the Persian Gulf carrying oil to the U.S., Western Europe, or Japan. When you consider the falling value of the dollar, and how many dollars go out of this country for the products and raw materials that we consume, then you can understand why foreign companies raise their prices for their goods that we buy with our dying dollar. This cost is all shifted to the shoulders of the American man on the street, who does the final buying of the finished product.

You and I pay the price daily for a falling dollar. It is beginning to hurt, and hurt badly.

Many Americans are cutting back on the quality of foods they once ate. Steak and the finer cuts of meat are no longer daily items of the average diet; cheaper cuts are far more popular today. Meat seasoners and tenderizers are more common than ever. Less and less expensive dishes are prepared by Mom these days, for Dad just cannot afford all that luxury the family used to enjoy.

Americans are holding onto their cars longer. There is not the turnover into new automobiles that there once was. Mechanics are busier than ever repairing and rebuilding the "older model" now that Dad is getting much more conservative.

A gallon of gasoline according to the latest predictions, will soon cost one dollar and more, catching up to our European neighbors, who pay over $1.50 per gallon in many countries.

The American loaf of bread will soon be over the dollar mark, for the ever-increasing costs of oil (which is the base for fertilization), as well as other energy needs in farming, raise the prices of farm products. You pay the increase. In some cases all levels of business suffer, from the farmer to the processor to the manufacturer to the retailer and finally to the consumer.

New homes are rising nearly $10,000 per year in value, and now the average young couple cannot afford the type of new house which had once been purchased by the average couple, with both working and making the average American salary.

Interest rates are high and going higher in a government monetary program to somehow cut back inflation. Higher interest rates mean less money for the man on the street to use for his home, improvements, car, or business advances.

Higher interest rates mean much tighter money situations for the businessman in big business. He cannot or will not afford the higher rate of interest, and therefore he will not expand his business, inventories, plants, or offices. He does not hire new help, skilled or unskilled, for expansion is unaffordable.

In many cases when money is tight because interest rates are high, businesses cut back on all kinds of development and even lay off employees, since they can coast on built-up inventories of products for some time, without manufacturing new ones. This creates greater unemployment, including more unemployed people on welfare roles and depleted unemployment insurance.

The Dying Dollar Affects Everyone Everywhere.

People are wearing clothes longer and buying less new ones. Vacations are shorter, and less money is being spent on holidays, food, pleasure, and recreation. Dollars have to be stretched further for more important items during the year. Much less money is spent overseas by traveling Americans. They have found that it is downright expensive to dine in a European hotel, since the American dollar has lost so much of its value in overseas purchasing power.

As the dollar goes down in value and quietly dies, we

all buy less and do less, and thus unemployment increases, for demand of service and supplies is not there, and there is a vicious circle producing worsening economic effects every week.

We are all aware that the dollar is dying, but few of us understand why, or how we can survive this death.

We hear of overseas economic dismay at our once-proud American dollar. During the last year the dollar lost 30 percent of its value against the Japanese Yen, 33 percent against the Swiss Franc, 15 percent against the German Mark, and varying amounts against other currencies worldwide. The Canadian dollar fared even worse, largely because it is so affected by the economics of the U.S. and the financial policies of the present government.

The OPEC nations—the oil-producing exporting countries—are all talking again about a price hike this coming winter on the price of a barrel of oil, because they say they are losing millions of dollars every week (if not every day) as the value of the American dollar goes down weekly.

The OPEC nations cannot afford to lose any longer. They are talking about using the new European money idea, recently surfacing after six European leaders and President Carter got together to discuss the precipitous fall of the American dollar, and what the President was going to do about it.

The net result was that the Europeans, tired of being battered daily in their own currency values related to the falling dollar, and not backed by the stability of gold, have decided to create their own new Eurocurrency, called "ECU"—European Currency Unit. It will be in competition with the dollar and will be supported by all the Common Market Countries. The ECU money will be used on the international level at first, for the carrying on of everyday trade and commerce between countries. It will eventually become the Common Market Currency, to be used by all nations in Europe as their only money. Monetary unity has been one of the goals of the Common Market countries since its inception in 1948. They have a large, power wielding committee working on this new money right now.

If the OPEC nations decide to dump the dying dollar as the determining value for the barrel of oil, the financial repercussions will be so strong that Wall Street may not be able to handle it. I predict a crash. I'll tell you why shortly.

The dollar has been the one monetary unit used, recognized, and respected by the nations of the world as the world monetary denominator: It has been the money of last resort and the determining factor in evaluating each nation's currency and the pricing of virtually all products. The dollar has been the only monetary unit in all of history to be adopted by the nations with such respect and used as the international reserve currency. Never before has this happened; we should be proud. But now the Europeans want to set up their own new currency, and dump the dollar from this prestigious position. By so doing, that could very well be the last act against the dying dollar—the thing that kills it completely!

Also, by setting up their own currency for the nations to use, the Europeans will have set up a monetary system of stability backed by gold, a system which would shield the world economy from the shocks and waves that have repeatedly come from basing the value of all currencies on the daily value of the dollar. There are too many ups and downs with the "snake"— the current title for Euro-monies. They wiggle up and down like a snake, primarily because of the falling of the dollar and their own reevaluation as a consequence of the actions of the American dollar.

If you regard the new ECU money from Europe biblically, and tie that into the "Electronic Fund Transfer System" being set up everywhere, you can readily realize what the Prophet John in Revelation was implying when he suggested that a final credit card would be stamped on every human, doing away with checks, cash, other credit cards of a losable type, and all monetary sytems of the nations, as they melted into the practicality of this new idea.

This system would tremendously lessen the burden on nations using all different kinds of currencies. It would ease the strain on banking, since all computations would be done through computers with "Digital Monetary Inputs" instead of checks, cash, dollars, and credit cards that have to be monitored.

Everyone could have his own number in his own Master Computer File, and any bank, business, government, or individual would have access to the computer. Anytime his number was used, anyone possessing the number would know his financial situation at once. He could not buy or sell, could not be a consumer or wholesaler or retailer, without his computerized number.

The new ECU money will be backed by the stability of gold. This is why all nations will use it.

We Americans are very aware of our dying dollar. The Europeans are disgusted with our dying dollar, and even the Arabs, who once loved the American dollar, are planning on using a monetary system with far greater stability. They are planning on dumping the dollar.

Some economists have said that this devaluation of the dollar is good for us. They state the well-known fact that as our dollar goes down, and our products are priced by the dollar, foreign investment is heavier in the U.S. immediately, since the overseas buyer gets more for his currency. But how much help is this? Do we really want foreigners buying up our land, our business and our homes? This might have a patchwork effect of helping ease the strain on our balance-of-payments deficit, but in the long run it will prove very unsatisfactory to Americans, who have not needed foreign ownership before and certainly don't want it now. The foreigners bought our products before the dollar started to die, and they will buy them again if we stabilize our dollar and bring worldwide respect for our currency again.

The dollar is diseased, and unless the proper surgery is performed immediately, it will die a horrible death and take its victims into the world's most terrible depression. It will be a time of great suffering for millions of Americans and others.

The American people, the ones who support the government with their hard-earned tax dollars, are the victims who will suffer the most from the diseased, dying dollar.

With consumer confidence in Washington's fiscal leadership at an all-time low, and with consumer spending power at an unprecedented minimum, and with no signs of the needed surgery forthcoming soon, the world is shaken, we are stricken, and the depression is on its way.

Chapter

2

The Real Killer

As in any murder plot or conspiratorial plan, the blame is shifted to everyone but the real culprit. Many times the real killer goes free.

In the insidious war on the dollar, the killer is the one you would suspect the least. You've often tried to solve the mystery on television, by predetermining who the killer was. Many times you were right, and many times you were wrong.

In the case of the death of dollar, there are several possibilities. You could blame it on the guest who was invited to stay for a long vacation—"the oil barons of the world"—the Arabs and their precious black gold. We could say that oil was the killer and that America's lust for energy and its insatiable appetite for fuel consumption has murdered the dollar by bringing about an unbalanced trade deficit—we import more goods than we export, and there is a wide difference between payments **to** us for our products, and payments **by** us for overseas products, especially oil.

But is oil the killer or the dollar? Certainly not. Americans have always consumed vast amounts of energy, in some cases more than the rest of the world combined, especially during the last forty years. The oil-exporting countries' investments in the U.S. and their purchases of our products almost offset their exports to the U.S.

Oil has not been a killer, but on the contrary has been the most valuable asset we have ever imported from abroad or discovered on our own continent, our offshore areas and Alaska. It is "black gold" for this country.

Oil-based products abound on every store shelf and in every home pantry. Oil is involved in virtually every action produced by energy forces in this country, from heating millions of homes to heating the blast furnaces of Pittsburgh, from producing energy for giant turbines which grind out electrical power to moving your car and the trucks and diesel trains that bring everyday products to your city.

Oil is not only necessary, but oil produces the biggest dollars this country makes, eclipsing every other product. No other natural resource or imported product produces nearly as much riches as oil.

Our insatiable hunger for oil and our multiplied uses of it create the biggest monthly expense for our domestic budget, to be paid by the consumers via the government, overseas and domestically. Oil is our largest expense and thus makes our balance-of-payments difficult to balance. But if our dollar were worth what it once was, without government interference in the marketplace, oil would not be creating the balance-of-payments deficit that it is now. If a dollar were still a dollar in its purchasing power, prices would be lower for overseas products. The foreign countries wouldn't be charging what they are currently forced to charge, for the dollar would still buy what it did before. But when the dollar drops in value, foreign products go up in price.

The dying dollar is the reason our imports of oil and other products cost so much more today. The disease is in the dollar—not in oil or imported products. Certainly they cost more, but only because our dying dollar purchases less and less. We will discuss why in a moment.

Back to the death scene and the real killer. Is it possible that the "son" is the killer of the "father dollar," the "son" being labor and big business in America?

Is it possible that their greed for gain and power, the multinational corporations have stuck the dagger into the dollar by wage and price hikes of an astronomical nature?

According to the best economists, wages and prices have gone up because the dollar has gone down. The diseased dollar is the **cause**, not the effect.

The President says, "Cut energy needs and big salaries and high costs in big business—those two things, and you will have no more inflation than what we can properly live with."

He is always placing the blame on the private business sector and the energy-consuming public for inflation and the death of dollar values. But neither one of these two alleged killers are the real culprits.

Certainly there are big-union abuses of their powers, and certainly there is much corruption in big business, and certainly there are powerful lobbyists in Washington pulling for "their thing" that takes much money. But there have always been white-collar criminals gouging the public, bilking the government, and pulling off schemes that produce millions in illegal, untaxed profits. These are "little foxes that spoil the grapes on the vine," but they are not the actual killers of the dollar. They nibble at it and annoy it, but America is too strong to let "energy" or "big business" be the real culprit. There is a powerful resiliency in the American dollar, a resiliency that can withstand the worst that "labor" or "energy needs" can throw at it. The killer is not these things at all. These are merely effects of the cause, and not the real cause of the death of our dollar at all.

The real killer is the "butler," as in all ancient plots. The "Butler" is the one who works the kitchen and keeps the house running well behind the scenes. He is a hired overseer in the house for the purpose of keeping the house in order as to its domestic needs, with some outside duties as well.

The "hired butler" is your government—the highly paid officials who are elected to keep our American house in order, domestically first of all, with some outside responsibilities to the rest of the world.

The federal government, with emphasis on the White House and its occupants, is the killer of the dollar of the United States. It is murdering your last dollar! The federal government may look innocent, but you will find that the overwhelming amount of experienced economic opinion points the finger at UNCLE SAM. Let me prove the point clearly.

Two major problems exist today with respect to political economics. First, the government is printing too much money weekly thus reducing the value of the dollar weekly in its purchasing power. This is pure inflation. Inflation of the currency means deflation of purchasing power for you and me. No wonder Milton Friedman just stated, "We're going to have a recession, and the later it happens, the deeper it will be." (**Sacramento Bee**, November 13, 1978).

At one time money production was related to gold holding, but this is no longer true; there are no gold restrictions on the flow of the currency.

Prior to gold backing the thought was that money should be increased only as the total goods and services of the country were increased, so that these goods and services could be utilized by the consumer. This is no longer true. The money supply is now partially dictated by the government's budget, and it is astronomical. You and I pay for this in increased taxation and higher prices.

The second major problem is so sinister and so fraught with mystery that no one wants to talk about it, and in fact 99 percent of the people know nothing about it. It is simply that our money-producing agency, the Federal Reserve System of banking, is not owned by the government of the United States. It is **privately** owned by international interests, and has been since before 1913. We only have a government-appointed 7-man liaison board acting in our government's interests. The privately owned system of the Central Bank (with its 12 regional banks) supplies the credit money and currency money to the local, domestically owned banks of the country.

This being true, the Central Bank can control, at its will and to its selfish benefit, the currency and credit expansion and contraction (directly and via interest rates) to the tune of billions. When they cautiously expand credit and currency (through direct printing or reduced interest rates), they expand business in the country through the expertise and hard work of the businessmen. When they call in their credit notes and demand currency payment from the businessman, and he finds himself unable to pay with cash, they can take over his business through foreclosure and add it to their already booming multinational business empires.

Through this expansion or contraction of business, the leaders of the Central Bank control prosperity and can produce depression. Are they part of an international confidence game with the banks of Europe too? Are they part of the plan to overthrow this government and Canada and force us into one-world government, with them at the head? Has our government committed the gravest of all errors by allowing private internationalists to control the flow of credit and currency in the United States? Do these men own the banks of England, France, Germany, Italy, the United States, etc., as indicated by knowledgeable sources? Are they planning on the death of the U.S. and the birth of the new world order soon, as indicated by G.C. Coogan and ratified by Senator Robert Owen (D-N.Y.) in the book, **Money Creators**? More on this later.

The government was originally authorized to use the monies brought in through legalized taxation of the working man and business profits. As long as the elected members of Congress voted for and planned programs valuable to the people of the United States, and kept those programs of aid, development, welfare, defense, education, etc. within the annual U.S. income, there would never be a deficit, the government would never go into debt. The money supply would not have to be increased to satisfy the monstrous demands of government.

But politicians have always wanted to spend more than they took in from taxes on profit and personal incomes. Consequently, many leaders have thoroughly detested having the dollar pegged to gold, for it brought fiscal restraint to some politicians who wanted to turn the crank of the money press, thereby flooding the market with dollars.

Pressure was brought to bear by insidious forces within the banking world, the Federal Reserve System, and organizations within the U.S. which were more interested in filling their own coffers and getting rich than in bettering the country. Gold was demonetized, the dollar was freed from its weighty anchor, and the printing presses started to roll.

The government wanted to spend more than its revenues would bring in, and the only two ways to get more money would be to print it, and/or to float government issued, triple-A-rated bonds, with a high interest rate to the public and to private business, and to soak up money from the marketplace at the same time. Though this would give the government more money to play with (future generations of taxed Americans could pay the money back to the generation loaning it), it also would soak up the maximum amount of money available to the private sector for business expansion and development. Then the man on the street wouldn't be able to find a bank or Savings and Loan to loan him the money he might need for personal reasons, since they would have loaned their available monies to the government at a higher interest rate than they could charge the local consumer. They were out to make money, so they got it from the government by loaning the government what they had, in exchange for the triple-A-rated government bonds. This hurt big and small business at various times when it was done. Production was cut back and many people were laid off, bringing slowdowns and even recessions in history at those times when the bonds were floated, and interest rates went higher.

But the easiest way to get money for the politicians (to buy votes in their areas of influence and to buy the power that comes from the dollar) was simply to print it.

Grow too many oranges, and the price of oranges will fall on the market. Produce too many cars (more than supply and demand really needs), and the price of cars will fall. Print too many dollars, and the value of the dollar will fall. Continue this printing of too many dollars, and you will have worldwide depression.

If the Fed shifted its policy of creating too much money, reducing its current yearly rate of 7.8 to 9 percent (or more) to only 2 percent **we could kill inflation virtually immediately.** It might create a slowdown temporarily, but that slowdown in the general economy would not last over 4 months, if that long, as the general public realized what value there was in this action. Psychologically, it would thrust new blood into the general marketplace. The stock market would soar at the knowledge that the government was cutting its money production by over 6 percent annually.

This would mean fewer government giveaway programs. It might hurt social programs, but that also might put some people right back to work, if they knew they were dropped from welfare payments.

Of the 3.4 million families on welfare rolls in 1975, more than 35 percent had been on welfare over 5 years. That's a total of 1.1 million families! In that group, 71,326 had been on relief **20 years or longer!** (See the **Chicago Tribune**, January 26, 1978.)

Cutting the money supply would undoubtedly hurt the power and influence which some senators and congressmen have in certain areas, as their personal programs might be curtailed. But it would be better for some local programs not to go through than to endanger the whole country because of politicians' promises to favorite constituents.

It is true that some programs might go unattended in local areas, and that our foreign aid and power-buying gifts and benefits to friendly nations would be cut back dramatically, and that Russia might take up the slack. But if we don't curtail our giveaways, if we don't restrain our domestic and foreign policy **now**, we won't be able to engage in any of these programs anyway. The depression will hit us, and it will all be over. Restraint **now** could keep us from depression and at the same time allow us to surge ahead economically. This would no doubt serve to sharpen congressional focus on programs that are really needy. Our priorities would be reappraised, and the emphasis would be placed **where the real needs are.**

The President has a budget for federal spending of 500 billion dollars for 1979. Even the President forecasts a 60-billion-dollar deficit, which is dangerously higher than that of any previous President. Many Republicans think the budget deficit will top 100 billion dollars and could well go to 150 billion dollars. This means a 150-billion-dollar debt **on top of** the multi-trillion-dollar-debt we already have!

Our President is spending too much money! His programs are too impractical, and in some cases far too generous when you consider the consequences to the country, as the money supply goes up and inflation rises still higher because of his programs.

"Our government is going through over one billion dollars every 24 hours, and that rate is rising. Furthermore, the interest alone on our national debt is running at just over $48 billion a year, all things considered." So says Johnny Johnson, creator and writer of the spirited **Daily News Digest**, P.O. Box 39027, Phoenix, Arizona. Write him for a copy of this Digest. It is tops.

There are now over 600 billion U.S. dollars in overseas hands. If our overseas friends get any more jittery about the value of the dollar or feel that it is going to die soon, then look out! When they start dumping dollars for gold (as they are doing now, as the U.S. auctions off its gold) or for other nation's currencies, then watch the dollar's value drop calamitously overnight. It could produce a depression.

Writer after writer in the economic advisory sector of our nation is telling us that the dollar is dying because of big government spending programs, requiring the printing of billions of unnecessary dollars and thereby killing their value.

Inflation is basically "too much money chasing too few goods." Governments produce printed "fiat" money for people to use. The government determines the money supply which is called M1 and M2 and is reported daily in the Wall Street Journal, among other papers.

Cut the money supply and there will be less money available. Eventually, after a short period of readjustment in the minds of people and the general marketplace of the entire nation, you will have fewer price hikes, and even prices coming **down**. Imagine prices coming down in virtually every product in the nation!

There would be a short period of decline, as long as 6 months or as short as 3 months, until both the business sector and finally the private consumer fully realized what was happening.

Less money immediately would mean less purchasing, and therefore some layoffs and less production on the part of business. But after 6 months at the most the country could be back on its feet, with lower prices everywhere, to the delight of the consumer. A short slowdown is far better than the killing of the dollar by overprinting and thereby the killing of the whole economy of the country.

Chapter

3

Is There a Conspiracy to Overthrow the Government Financially?

Bankers became political barons when banking first came into being. We can thank Meyer Amchel Rothschild, founder of the Bank of England, for the establishment of the international banking system. After establishing his banking empire in England, he placed his son Carl over the Bank of Naples in Italy, his son James over the great Bank of France, his son Edmund over the Bank of Germany, his son Solomon over the Bank Of Vienna, and his son Nathan over the Bank of England.

Meyer once made the statement, "Give me the power to coin money and set its value, and I care not who makes the laws."

From this statement comes a conspiracy to neutralize the governments of the Western world and force them into a one-world government system via the destruction of their currencies and the establishment of a new world monetary unit for all nations to use.

The original banks of Europe took the names of the countries in which they existed. People felt that the banks represented the government after a period of time, but they did not! The same is true in America. Many Americans believe that the Federal Reserve

Banks, owned and operated by the Federal Reserve, belong to the Federal Government completely. They do not! They are owned and operated by private individuals who are part of an international corporation of the world's richest men. Who knows who owns the Federal Reserve System, where the money is printed? Do you? Do you know of any list of men anywhere? Why the secrecy?

These men who own and run the Federal Reserve System also run and control the 12 regional banks for the System in the United States, those banks that loan out money to the other privately owned and government-owned banks. What a privilege!

These unbelievably rich men, who own the system of printing money for the United States, control the banking industry of this and many other countries. They can wield a power that is unbelievable, unpredictable, and totally unimaginable. Just remember that our United States Government borrows money from the Fed with its triple-A-rated bonds, bought up by the Fed. We pay interest on these bonds, and we pay off the bonds with taxpayers' money! Who are we paying this money to? Who are these men who can garner off the wealth of this country and control depressions and recessions and inflation and deflation by the punching of keys in their powerful computers? These private individuals, in conjunction with the federal government, determine financial principles that run the country economically.

According to the latest and most valuable information secured by this writer, the Council on Foreign Relations, set up originally by a Colonel Edward House in 1919 (located at 68th Street and Park Avenue in New York City), is a powerful organization of over 1725 members to date which controls the foreign and much of the domestic policy of the United States.

The organization was originally set up from a meeting held in Paris to study international affairs. It was to be funded from the Rockefeller, Carnegie, and Ford Foundations. Later, multinational corporations supported the CFR.

It was the CFR, along with other important factors, that maneuvered our entry into World War II. It was members of the CFR that originally helped finance the Bolshevik Revolution in Russia with American dollars from American banking interests in New York City. They also set up the model for the one-world govern-to unite the world into a one-world-government. They member Alger Hiss wrote the charter, and John D. Rockefeller provided the land for the United Nations headquarters to be built in the United States.

The Council on Foreign Relations has a network of intelligence men in every vital spot of the earth. Their communications network for what was going on everywhere in foreign-policy-making appeared to be flawless. They wanted to control the foreign-policy-making of the United States government, and have virtually succeeded. Almost every Secretary of State, Deputy Secretary of State, Secretary of Defense, Secretary of the Treasury, National Security Advisor, and Director of the Central Intelligence Agency, as well as many other key positions since the Eisenhower Administration, has come from the CFR. Over 75 percent of the men nearest the President today have come through the CFR or related organizations set up by the CFR since its inception.

The CFR soon realized that the United Nations, which they helped to set up, was not the organization to unite the world into a one-world government. They dropped the idea of setting up a world government along territorial lines, and are now organizing a world government along more functional lines, via world monetary systems and political control that comes through owning the banks and controlling each country's currency operations, as it does the United States through the Federal Reserve System.

Europe developed its own CFR, known as the Bilderbergers, later on. Made up of money barons, multinational corporation leaders, bankers, politicians, etc., the Bilderbergers came into existence to guide the destiny of the European nations financially and to control them politically through financial manipulation.

What the Bilderbergers are to Europe, the CFR is to the United States. The latest offshoot of these organizations, one which also includes the blossoming economic power of the Far East in Japan, is the newly formed Trilateral Commission.

As the Rockefellers controlled interests in both of the former organizations, so David Rockefeller was chosen to set up this new one.

In 1973 the Trilateral Commission was set up by inviting leaders of the banking world from America, Europe, and Japan to form an organization together with politicians, powerful multinational corporation executives, and media executives. Jimmy Carter, Walter Mondale, and many others became members. Zbigniew Brzezinski was its first chairman, and he is now our National Security Advisor!

At this time we have have the following Trilateral and CFR men involved in the leadership of our country and its policies in the financial, domestic, and international realms: Jimmy Carter, our President; Walter Mondale, our Vice-President; Zbigniew Brzezinski, Assistant to the President on National Security Affairs; Michael Blumenthal, U.S. Secretary of the Treasury; Henry Kissinger, Vice Chairman of the Advisory Board for Chase Manhattan Bank; Sol Linowitz, Negotiator of the Panama Canal Treaties; Paul Nitze, U.S. delegate to the SALT talks; Nelson Rockefeller, Chairman of the Rockefeller Brothers Fund; Paul Warnke, Director of the U.S. Arms Control and Disarmament Agency; Cyrus Vance, U.S. Secretary of State; Robert Anderson, Chairman of the Board of the Atlantic Richfield Company, Federal Reserve Bank of New York; J. Paul Austin, Chairman of the Board for the Coca Cola Company; Eugene Black, American Express Company; Emilio Collado, Executive Vice-President of Exxon Corporation; Hedley Donavan, Editor in Chief of Time Magazine; Jacques Fouchier, President of Banque de Paris; Henry J. Heinz, Chairman of the Board of H.J. Heinz Co. From overseas, representation from the Orient and Europe includes the President of the Sumito Bank, Japan; President of the Nippon Steel Company; President of the Bank of Tokyo; Chairman of the Hitachi Company; President of the Sony Corporation; President of the Mitsubishi Bank; the President of the Bank of Belgium, who is a Director of the Exxon Company; President of the Toyota Company; Chairman of Royal Dutch Petroleum; Edward Rothschild, President Compagnie Financaire Holding; Chairman of Sears, Roebuck and Company; the U.S. envoy to Communist China; and many other illustrious figures in the world of business and politics.

It appears to me, from all that has been printed on these three organizations that they are bent on producing a one-world government. They want unity instead of political diversification, which sounds very good. They plan on monetary unity for all nations participating in their world government. That international monetary system will be backed by gold, which many of them hold great possessions of. When gold **really** climbs (as it will) and becomes the backer of the new world currency, those holding it will become the richest people on earth. Those without it will be subservient to those with it.

When this one-world government is set up, it will be headquartered in Europe and will have control over all energy and oil production, over all food production and distribution, and over the use of most of the world's money.

Can you imagine the political promises made by the leaders of this movement to the ones whose support they are now attempting to gain? How many world leaders in high political positions have been promised higher positions and greater power and financial rewards for their support than they have ever dreamed of?

The Bilderbergers were set up after the Council on Foreign Relations, and, like the CFR, they have been dominated by the Rockefeller family quite strongly until lately. Originally they were drawn together by the efforts of the Rockefellers along with the leadership of Prince Bernhard of The Netherlands at the Bilderberger Hotel of Oosterbeek, Holland, during the last week of May, 1954.

In a most recent meeting (their 26th) the Prince was missing because he is thoroughly embarrassed after being exposed on the world's front pages for taking huge payoffs from Lockheed for favors rendered to them and then squandering these millions which he received illegally. He may have been dropped by now from the prestigious position he once held in the Bilderbergers.

The Bilderbergers even denied their own existence for a year after their organizational meeting in 1954. They meet in utmost secrecy, with heavily armed guards always visibly present. They are made up of many of the world's wealthiest bankers, richest industrialists, and most powerful politicans. With their 100 or so members present in the last meeting, which took place in Princeton, New Jersey, April 20-23, 1978, they represent the highest single concentration of investment capital in history! It is said that the Bilderbergers form the nearest thing to a powerful world secret government. Being internationalists, and being multinational in their representation, they comprise the type of powerful leaders that could plunge the world into economic depression and force the world (in order to eat and survive) to join their plan for the one-world government. These meetings provide the atmosphere of extreme secrecy which enables Rockefeller to meet in private sessions with Baron Edmund and Baron Guy Rothschilds to discuss world economic affairs and their plans for world currencies, multinational corporations they control, and anything else you could imagine. This is where the magnates of German, Swedish, and Italian banking meet with Canadian and American and British counterparts to discuss world trade, banking, and the dollar's woes and future. Everyone imaginable was present in Princeton.

Henry Kissinger led the Rockefeller delegation along with David Rockefeller. They arrived in bulletproof limousines surrounded by escort vehicles full of bodyguards fingering machine guns. White House security advisor Zbigniew Brzezinski arrived with a five-man secret service escort along with General Haig, supreme commander of NATO.

These and many other representatives from megabanks, industry, and politics met in absolute secrecy.

But one great leak came from the meeting. **They discussed the inevitability of the coming crash. A worldwide depression is on its way!** This was the grim word given to all members. You can be assured that they discussed this crash and how to turn it to their own economic advantage.

The charge is leveled by many who appear to be in the know that these organizations are attempting to do the following things as quickly as possible:

1. Form a one-world government with its leadership based in Europe.
2. Through these powerful leaders control food development and distribution throughout the cooperating nations.
3. Control oil and energy development and distribution.
4. Produce and control a gold-based monetary system for all nations to use, and then dump the dollar.
5. Help many nations become equal sharers in the benefits of the richer nations.

Right now, these men have the power to force politicians in their direction by the money-power they control in Europe, America, and Japan.

They have the power to raise interest rates, make money tight, produce recessions or depressions, devalue currencies on the international money markets, sell out a currency completely in less than a week, release much money for business use, tighten the reins on local governments, and twist the arms of leaders in powerful positions who do not agree with them. They can even manipulate wars by helping to finance opposing sides to their own advantage making much money from the wars they finance.

These men sell scientific expertise to the Soviets and the Chinese Communists as long as it benefits their financial interests. They build big factories in Russia and equip them with American science and technological know-how, and then give efficient training to the Soviets to build trucks, cars and machines with American expertise. Then we have to compete with our own developed technology on the international markets for the trucks and industrial products the Russians build! Here in America we have companies that are now buying Soviet trucks made exactly this way, thanks to the multinational Americans who sold us out to the Soviets!

Some of these power barons even finance guns and other pieces of military equipment to be sold indirectly to the enemy through other nations and corporations, to be used against our own soldiers. This was done in the Vietnam War.

We are now starting a program of doing the same things with the Chinese Communists, who hate us and all that we stand for, but who will use us to their own end by gaining valuable scientific benefits, products, computers, oil-drilling machinery, and even materials and products that could be used against us in an all-out war.

It appears that some men can never get enough; greed makes for more greed. They are never satisfied with the immense riches they have already accumulated; they must have more. They have the most voracious, rapacious, insatiable hunger for money and the power it brings. They could never possibly use all their money in their lifetime. Nor could their families or relatives.

There is a sinister, satanic greed and lust in the hearts of these extremely rich world leaders in industry, banking, media, and politics. They are led by forces from out of this world.

This is the overall satanic plot to destroy the better plans of good men and to thwart the plan of God for mankind forever.

Satan exists; there isn't any doubt about it. Biblical accounts indicate that he was a powerful archangel, having one third of the angels in heaven under his jurisdiction, as did his two counterparts, Michael and Gabriel.

Lucifer fell, due to pride and wanting to become greater than God. He took a third of the angels with him to the earth, and they became the demonic forces of hell that drive men today to do evil.

Satan, as he was later called, entered into a threefold plan to destroy the plan of God for mankind.

First, he planned to keep the human race in heathenistic ignorance and superstition. He succeeded to an extent. Even today, after hundreds of years of evangelism, missionary activity, and humanitarian efforts to alleviate the heathen from their tragic conditions sociologically and theologically, we still have India's teeming millions deep in superstition, ignorance, and false religious philosophies. Africa, Japan, and the Far East are steeped in religions that never did a thing except rob the people of their freedoms, money, dignity, and self-respect.

Secondly, Satan produced another evil worse than the first. He could not conquer all of mankind with heathenism, so he brought about Communism. Now one-third of the world is under the control of communistic power and is moaning under the cruel fate of it all, while many millions are butchered by the same evil philosophy today in Cambodia, Laos, South Vietnam, and other places. China butchered her millions under Mao, and Russia murdered her millions under Stalin and his bloodthirsty successors. They are all without God, without Christ and His teachings, and without freedom.

Everywhere Christianity went, it brought freedom, equality, and liberty, plus the free-enterprise system eventually.

Now we have the last of the three plans in the satanic plot. Most of the world would not accept heathenism, and millions would not accept Communism, so Satan planned to enslave them through the thing they pride the most—their money and their capitalistically gained possessions.

Create confusion in their monetary systems. Bring greed and distrust from nation to nation among them. Add great doses of jealousy over what one nation has that the other doesn't. Mix all this with wars over territorial gains, oil, and energy. Add wild ideas about independence and freedom even among those who are free, like Quebec, the blacks, the gays, the Women for Equal Rights Amendments, the Irish, the ambitious Black nations of Africa, the Palestinians, and the political anarchists in South and Central America. Then, while the people rise up in guerrilla armies to overthrow their dictators, their leaders, and their governments, and while saboteurs plan political assassinations and achieve them in the largest of the free countries, lead them into demonetization of their gold and silver, as did Rome. Then watch them fall into such mass confusion and into such a worldwide capitalistic depression that their only recourse will be to join the satanic leaders' plan for a world takeover through money.

Have you ever taken a good look at the whole picture put together? We usually see it in parts, and for most of us it is difficult to put the clandestine results of these meetings together. They have made it a clever puzzle so that we cannot understand it.

The following piece of my imagination is presented as a fictitious scenario that could well be true. It is the dynamic hypothetical story of a reporter who got into a Bilderbergers meeting. The European leaders had invited the members of the Council on Foreign Relations and the Trilateral Commission to share in these study sessions for world peace and prosperity.

Perhaps not all members of these organizations fully understand what is really going on, and what the final role of these organizations will really be. But they will become enlightened. In the meantime they are invited members because they have either money, political power, experience, or knowledge in certain fields, or else they have the charisma necessary to help put the program over to the nations once the day arrives.

The following is an imaginary story that presents these facts:

Having a good friend in Washington politics in a rather high position on the President's Cabinet enabled me to learn one night that a rather clandestine meeting was going to be held some four months away in a large, protected, luxury hotel in the United States.

Upon further inquiry that evening, while plying my political friend with tongue-loosening alcohol, I learned that it was a highly secret, extremely important meeting of the European Bilderbergers group, along with the executive members of the Council on Foreign Relations and certain department heads, plus the highest members of the Trilateral Commission from Europe, Japan, the U.S., and Canada.

There were to be no Presidents, Prime Ministers, Kings, or Queens present, but a most highly selected group of the barons of the world's banks, industries, publications, and governments were to be present. There was to be absolutely no press coverage, but plenty of guards, guns, and dogs to maintain absolute secrecy. There would be no press reports coming out of the meeting. It would be the greatest gathering of financial-political-powerhouses in all of world history.

My friend in the White House had seen a private memo secreted into one of the President's men indicating who would be at the meeting, and noting that this man (one of the President's right-hand men) was of course invited and was assured of strict privacy concerning his attendance. The memo also noted that it was to be destroyed immediately. This Cabinet member was a member of the Trilateral Commission.

Needless to say, apart from my wife, who was sworn to secrecy and who shared my interest in this meeting with an indescribable keenness, no one knew of my intentions to bug it and get in somehow. I only told her about my intentions in case something "unfortunate" happened to me.

I knew the hotel fairly well, having been to a previous convention within its auspicious walls.

I checked in for one week, two months before the meeting was to be held. I spent every day studying the walls and corridors; at nights, when the maintenance crews were at a minimum, I crawled through elevator shafts and air-conditioning ducts, checking every possible way to bug that giant convention room.

Knowing that they would "debug" the room electronically, I finally realized that there was only one way to get the information: I had to be there; I had to get in that meeting somehow.

There was no way I could cloak-and-dagger myself into the room; the security measures were too great. Everyone was to be checked out of the hotel who would be staying there within 24 hours of the meeting. All cooks, maids, butlers, and waiters were to be brought in from the staffs of these men. Everyone was part of the program, or else he was not allowed into the building at all! Never had I seen security so tight.

Many hours before the meeting was to convene, I crawled into my much-arranged "hole in the wall" through the return-air ventilation system, and propped myself up in a space about as big as the center portion of an office desk. My legs had very little room for motion, and my bottom was propped up by two of the softest pillows Sears ever sold!

I had two pillows for my back, plus pens, pencils, and a notebook the size of a small textbook.

My wife had assisted me in my toiletries and food package. I had two thermoses of water, vitamins, cheese, chocolates, and some small sandwiches that would last me two days if necessary. If I had to stay longer I was going to be in terrible trouble. I had Kleenex for bathroom purposes and a plastic container for excrement and urine. "People have survived for days on end without any of these things," my wife encouragingly told me.

"Besides," she added, "a good fast will clean your system and make a new man of you."

I had gotten into the hotel after-hours, and before any special security forces arrived. I waited for my long crawl until the last people were being "evicted" from their suites. My crawl would take me more than 150 feet down a shaft in total darkness. But I had already accomplished this feat once before in preparation for this day.

I slept the first night while our distinguished guests were checking in from points all over the world. Police and armed guards were checking everywhere. I could hear them talking below me and above and alongside. The room I was peering into was vast, and could accommodate at least a thousand people. It was set up in table style, with each man having room to study pre-arranged notes. In one area headphones were set up for interpreters to translate for those not fully understanding English.

By rearranging myself away from the vent that looked into the room, I could sleep stretched-out, and did so.

The next morning there was a very official roll call, a preview of the order of events to be discussed, further committees to be heard from, and a welcome speech to all by the presiding Prince from Belgium, head of the European organization of the Bilderbergers.

As the day went on, reports were made from the podium clearly pointing out to me that this organization had invited the other two organizations to be present to sum up what had been done toward bringing the nations of the world into alignment with their plan for a one-world-government society.

The committee on energy reported; the committee on world monetary union reported on ECU; a series of speakers spoke on the strength or weakness of their own nations' currencies and what to expect; it was shocking.

A committee on the World Food Bank spoke about world starvation and plans for world distribution of foodstuffs from America, Canada, Australia, and Argentina.

Another and another committee reported. The day crept into the evening session and was broken up only by short intervals for dining. Finally, after the evening session, all adjourned to meet at 7 o'clock the next morning for a full-day session to be climaxed by the special report from the Trilateral Commission Executive Department on what to expect in America.

My bones ached, my pills were gone, my sandwiches had been long-devoured, and my water was running out. So was my bladder, but I managed somehow. I remained in some pain, but I was thoroughly intrigued and completely undetected. I had removed everything metal from my person, not wanting metal detectors to pick up artificial elements present. I slept reasonably well during the night.

The final session came. I had been in purgatory now for almost three complete 24-hour periods. I had myriads of notes on names and countries.

After tributes were made to various members for works of excellence in furthering the cause of world relief through the philosophy of these three world bodies, and after motions were made concerning various uses of the news media, including radio, television, magazines, and newspapers for the great day coming, the final message (prepared in an every-member form) was distributed, and the Executive Director of the Trilateral Commission took the platform and spoke.

Each member of this august body had, in his own native language, a copy of the prepared text.

By listening to its reading, which fortunately for me was in English, I give it to you in its unwashed, uncensored form.

> GENTLEMEN: Getting directly to the point, I give you succinctly the history of our movements to date and the immediate plans for the implementation of our ultimate goal for the nations. We are closer to the goals than ever before in our illustrious history. We have had many setbacks and many encouragements, but have had tremendous determination. This is why we are all where we are today. Read with me silently the text I have prepared to bring you up-to-date point-by-point. We can go over this text point-by-point as you wish to question it after the reading. Shall we proceed.
>
> 1. Internationally banking was set up not only for the benefit of the people locally but for the furtherance of world unity, cutting across national borders and through national legislation to help bring the nations to the point of unity in one-world government through the use of their monetary systems.
> 2. Organization of our megabank systems with

leaders of the world politically—industrialists and men of the media to deal with international problems—has been accomplished through our three organizations to date.

3. In dealing with national differences, policies, and diverse philosophies of the whole world, we have achieved great unity with most of them.

4. We set up the United Nations for the implementation of our goal for the United States of the Western world to unite, but they have failed us, and have become merely a sounding board for many nations and a spectacle of debate and disunity.

5. We have even worked for the development of Communism in Russia and the Far East in order to bring about a parity among the nations that would keep them fighting to achieve this equality. So far we have succeeded in keeping the major powers from fighting between capitalism and Communism. We have gained the respect of the Communist leaders and the control we wanted over the capitalist leaders. They are in our hand.

6. We must not forget about the ideological differences of the Russians and of the Chinese Communists with one another and with the West. Fundamentally, they are all lovers of money and of world power. However, we have assured them that they will govern what they have, and much more, in the new world unity. We do not want to govern countries internally at all. We can control the masses through them, and the Western leaders. As you know, through the genius of our executive leaders here, we have and are gaining more and more control over 80 percent of the areas of the world producing the most needed world goods. This is our greatest achievement

until now. We need the friendship and loyalty of the Communist leaders first. They will need money, science, development, organizing, research, and assurance that we in this new world effort will include them in dividing up the world pie with them. Let them govern as they might in their own regimes; we only want to control them. They will be putty in our hands.

7. We arranged detente next, with much trade and help going to the Russians from American government leaders and private enterprises, especially in the United States and Europe.

8. Then came the SALT talks—strategic-arms-limitation-talks between the Soviets and the Americans—our military master stroke. The SALT talks have resulted in the Americans cutting back on their great lead in weaponry and allowing the Soviets to catch up and pass them. They too were to cut back, but they refused to do so. This was and is being planned by our men who are members of the Council on Foreign Relations and the Trilateral Commission, and who are members of our President's cabinet this very hour.

9. We have set up the same program with China's new, not-so-intransigent leaders, Hua and others, so that we can help them achieve parity-equality with the Western world. This will alleviate the threat of war. Give them what they want without war, so that they will not go to war.

10. Now that we are achieving parity with the Soviets and the Western world, and China is fitting into the new world of reality, we must work on speeding up equality and a greater sense of unity between the two giants we represent (the Bilderbergers and the Council on Foreign Rela-

tions speaking through their new voice, the Trilateral Commission, which also includes Japan). We must bring Europe and the North American continent together quickly if we are going to have one-world government in the decade of the 80's.

11. While we work on political levels and through detente and SALT, we enact the metric system into the Dominion of Canada and into the U.S.A. By bringing the metric system of Europe into Canada and the U.S.A., we will hasten the hour when the grass-roots level of society will notice little difference from Europe in the way they are governed.

12. While facing the reality of the risk of war with the Soviet Union (but all the while helping to build the Soviets in a state of equality with the Western world), we try to ward off the Soviet war with North America by negotiations, manipulations, and buying off the leaders.

13. Our secret meetings with Soviet leaders are always going on (by members of the CFR and Bilderbergers) to keep the Soviet giant appeased, and to watch from another vantage point what they are doing. They are always a threat to this world government in the minds of our men of these world bodies.

14. While other members of the committees handle details of plans, solving problems and implementing legislation, we set up the plan for the leaders of the IMF to bring about a demonetization of gold and silver from Western monetary systems and currencies. They succeeded in dumping gold from the dollar and other European currencies and silver from the coins, thus implementing a very important piece of legislation.

15. Now, by twisting arms and feeding false information to the leaders of finance in the United States and other countries, we cause their currencies to flounder up and down in utter monetary confusion.

16. We encourage expensive government programs for the people and for the world. We arrange great grants to Israel, Egypt, and other countries to keep peace in the Middle East or to bring it about. We arrange enormous financing for huge American corporations that might fail, thus making mandatory an increase in the printed paper money supply daily. We make sure there are big programs to be financed. We subsidize farmers, increase welfare payments, enlarge educational grants, and make great loans to ailing cities like New York.

17. We turn on the federal presses and print billions of dollars, eventually rendering the dollar useless.

18. We get the government to believe that by selling out all their gold from Fort Knox they can stabilize the dollar that is failing every week and sometimes every day.

19. We must buy up all the gold through our subsidiary organizations, so that the true buyers are not known. When we have the gold and silver bought up as much as possible, and have at the same time manipulated the sell-out of South Africa for her gold and diamonds on a civil-rights platform, then we will suddenly sell out all our stocks in the New York and European markets. We will do this virtually overnight, preferably on a Thursday and Friday, thereby taking advantage of the weekend. We will do this at a time when the markets have not fallen on their own yet, and

prices are still reasonably high.

20. We will bring about the complete fall of the dollar by having already moved out of the continental United States and Canada, and thus out from the observing eyes of government and the power of the banking regulations. Instead, we will set up banking offices in Panama, the Cayman Islands, and the Bahamas.

21. It may be necessary for us to act in a way that seems unpatriotic. Our actions, if detected, will look destructive. But we will proceed. The end result will be a one-world monetary system and a one-world government that all of us will share together.

22. When all parts of our multifaceted program are ready in Europe and in the United States, we will dump our holdings of billions of dollars on the market within a two-day period, selling all our stock and government bond holdings in every nation we represent. Overnight we will have a worldwide depression. All stock will be virtually worthless; currencies will be worth little more than the paper they are printed on; the countries will be in shambles. Complete depression will hit the Western world over the weekend.

23. We must make sure that we hold the gold, silver, and utility stocks in our hands, and that we buy up all the coal mines in Europe and North America.

24. This total overnight confusion will produce a breakdown in industry, educational systems, local and state governments, and the federal government. Unions will strike, and transportation will stop in the air and on land. Food shortages will set in, and energy shortages will immediately be apparent, for this action on our part will come in the dead of January-February winter.

25. Violence and anarchy will fill the big cities. Only those with some stored food and water, as well as gold and silver will make it. Others depending on weekly salaries and government checks (56% of Americans) will be at a loss. Government money will hardly be honored at all. Local proprietors usually cashing checks will be reluctant to do so.

26. Banks will close temporarily. Government-issued money will be useless as it is dumped on the world markets, and there will be such an abundant supply of it internationally that it will buy little at home and nothing abroad. No nation will want American money (or Canadian for that matter). Other nations' currencies also may collapse immediately, or may linger slightly longer until we manipulate their demise in a similar manner.

27. There will be a run on the banks Monday through Friday the following week, necessitating their closing immediately. If only 18 percent of Americans go to the banks and demand their savings, it will bankrupt the entire banking system and the dollar. In addition to what we are going to do, this will be the final straw, totally destroying the dollar.

28. Crime will not be stopped. Normally-well-behaved citizens will take to robbing neighbors who seem to have more. Murder will be the rule of the day within three weeks after the stock market crashes. Government policing agencies will be powerless to stop looting, stealing, robbery, and aggravated assault. Local law-enforcement officials will try to maintain peace but will be successful only as long as they too have food to eat and water to drink. The officials could also become abusive.

29. The National Guard will be called out to police the

nation and help distribute medical and food supplies to emergency areas. Units will set up eating stations, hospitals will be jammed, and mass confusion will bring a state of paralysis to America and Canada. Both will share similar banking, food, crime and anarchy fates, as well as similar government actions.

30. Those people who hold possessions in real estate will try to sell them for peanut prices to eat and live. Those who hold small fortunes in gold and silver will certainly survive. Local grocers, if they have any food left at all during the violence and looting, will take gold and silver coins for food. Only a small fraction of the American population has secured any of these coins and bullion—not enough to do any harm to our plans.

31. The U.S. Government will have sold all its gold and silver possessions by then. It will be powerless to redeem the value of its own dollar.

32. We know that the government plan is to initiate the widespread distribution of the new U.S. paper money, which is already printed and stored. But this will be of little value in the long run, for it will only appease the people temporarily, until they realize that there is nothing backing this new money, even as there was no gold to back the old dollar. At this point they will not even have the gross national productivity to talk about backing the dollar. All will be at a standstill.

33. We know that the people of America have great built-in resiliency to spring back. They became the greatest nation in the world in 200 years because of their ability to endure, work, and have a vision. The free-enterprise system works in producing and reproducing a work force, necessities, profit and a good living style. The Americans will

recover quickly.

34. However, before the Americans recover, they will have emergency martial law imposed by the government. The president will swing with us into the new-world government with headquarters in Europe as we give assurances of our help, aid, food, and continued flow of oil, which we will control as soon as we involve our oil magnates in the Trilateral Commission.

35. There is no need to fight wars. America will have to give up her world policing action and civil rights course for the rest of the world while she picks up her own pieces and gets herself back on her feet. Russia will not have to fight to conquer. She can be a part of the new social order where she is, with what she controls and even more. We do not want to have to govern remote sections of the world. The Soviets have agreed to participate with us for a larger piece of the world pie. They have our agreements on this. Africa will belong to the Soviets, and so will parts of Eastern Europe.

36. China poses no threat to us. She has promised to cooperate in this European world government as long as it does not interfere with her legitimate rights to the world she occupies. Trade will flourish between Europe and China, and Japan will have supervision over China's development. We will watch her growth and control her militarily. Mutual understanding will bring about a socialistic world far more quickly than war, far more wisely, and far more cheaply.

37. Israel knows little of what we are doing but will cooperate completely. Our plan includes guaranteeing the borders of Israel for at least seven years, with our NATO forces ensuring peace there. A place will be made for the Palestin-

ians in the area of the West Bank and Sinai. They will have autonomy and self-government immediately.

38. India and neglected parts of Africa will be self-reliant, with the programs to be implemented in these areas when we are in operation. Each nation will be brought to a new dimension of self-reliance, self-esteem, and cooperation with our United European Headquarters.

39. For our present course, we will continue our devaluation of the dollar through megabank manipulation. Federal reserve pressures will print billions of dollars, depressing them daily in value. Ever-expanding government programs of spending will require ever more dollars to be printed. Those of you in Europe, continue to buy and use the dollars, and soon you will get the word to dump them overnight for your own nations' currencies. Continue to buy the auctioned gold from the United States and from gold sales in South Africa. This is important.

40. The committee on ECU development has handed us their report indicating that they are ready to dump the IMF (International Monetary Fund), and that they are ready to utilize our vast computerized system in banking circles for the new digital computer inputs, called ECU (European Currency Units). It appears that unity in the use of ECU will not come until the actual day when stocks are sacrificed, banks are closed, and certain expendable currencies are dumped on the market to die. We will give you word of that day approaching. Everything will have to be done worldwide and simultaneously. Shortly thereafter, each nation will be using ECU in Europe. It will only be a few months until the

Americans will be using it as well. Their new money will lose steam in about six months as we treat it the same way as the current American dollar.

41. Now, gentlemen, as we begin to speed up the Federal printing presses in America and sell the rest of government-held gold in useless auctions to support the dying dollar, and increase our government spending programs as already secretly outlined to those of you in the current U.S. government and present Washington administration, sit tight. The moment of victory for us is at hand. In only about 24 months, the day we have long dreamed of will be here. Prepare yourselves: Do your homework, safeguard your interests at home, and begin to decide who from among us today in this auspicious group of world statesmen will serve on the executive committee and who our chairman will be. We will keep you informed through our media personnel representing us here today. From time to time messages will come to you of things not printable.

42. Your continued economic actions in England, Italy, and Denmark will only help us as you debauch their currencies and economics. With Germany holding fast, along with our savings department of Switzerland, we will rebuild England, Italy, and the other nations in Europe by the secure strength of Germany.

Mr. Chairman, I move that this meeting be adjourned.

Though the exact setting of the foregoing story is wholly hypothetical, I believe that the information presented is factual insofar as it presents truths related to the dollar, America, and the formulation of the one-world government.

Adding to the truths stated above in scenario form, a recent newspaper report stated:

> The principal culprits in the wrecking of the U.S. currency seem to be the megabanks themselves, which are now being investigated by the government for speculating against the dollar in foreign exchange markets. The megabanks have acted ruthlessly and self-destructively against their own national money in the international markets. It is common knowledge in Europe that the biggest Wall Street houses own the largest amounts of "short positions" on the dollar. The New York banks have bet the biggest sums against the rise or the stability of the dollar.
>
> With an exhibition of unscrupulous greed, these bankers have engaged in skimming off billions in crooked profits by practicing profiteering over patriotism. Some of the leading names in New York billionaires profited this way to the detriment of the country, including Rockefellers, Mellons, etc.
>
> Many Europeans are shocked by the actions of these bankers and multinational corporation holders.
>
> I am wondering how many of these megabank owners and multinational corporation presidents of long-standing big-business interests in the U.S. also have their hand in the Federal Reserve System (which controls the expansion and contraction of the credit and money supply for the country), thus ultimately bringing the U.S. and other nations (including Canada and Europe) to their economic knees and forcing us into the new world government.

You can readily see that our banks, dealing in self-interest policies, are greatly affecting the dollar weekly. They are driving the Europeans into ECU—even more quickly than they originally planned. Word has it that by March ECU will hit the world trade markets. It could be devastating for the dollar.

Interestingly enough, Chase Manhattan Bank and Citicorp have moved out of the country lately in branch offices outside the regulatory supervision of agencies of the U.S. government. They have especially used Panama as an area where they promptly engaged in overseas ventures accounting for more than half—56 percent—of all of Chase's total earnings. By the mid 1970's, Citicorp had fully 70 percent of its total earnings originating overseas.

Is it true that these banks sell and buy our currency when it pleases them, and exchange it for the currencies of other nations when it becomes financially acceptable, regardless of what this will do to the American dollar at home and abroad? This appears to be so.

And when you consider the facts of the preceding scenario about energy-related products, isn't it interesting that the Rockefellers are buying up every coal mine they can get their hands on?

In adding further fuel to this fire and really adding weight to the whole idea, Antony Sutton states in the **Trilateral Observer:**

> The basic Trilateral Commission structure is a power pyramid. At the tip of the pyramid we can identify a "financial mafia" compromising several old-line American families, the American aristocracy. Below this highest level is the Ex-

ecutive Committee for the U.S., linked to members of Executive Committees in Europe and Japan. Next comes the Trilateral Commission itself: 109 members from North America, 106 from Europe, and 74 from Japan. Trilaterals control the executive branch of the U.S. government, and so control policy. An ongoing program or project is to dominate 9 core countries in Europe (and Japan), and by virtue of their productive ability account for 80 percent of the world output! The "core" group can then dominate the remaining 20 percent of the world. The American multinationals provide country-by-country liaison, intelligence, and conduits, the sinews to bind a global New World Order, to the directions of the "financial mafia."

Sutton says that the Trilaterals have rejected the U.S. Constitution and the democratic political process, and that their objective is to obtain the wealth of the world for their own use under the pretense of "public service."

By controlling so much of the world's goods and produce, plus gold, silver, and utilities, they hold politicians in the palm of their hand in many cases. Money is power today. It is not difficult to see who holds the political power of the world.

Remember that many of the "captains" of world finance and "kings" of world government are often in two separate world camps. The "captains" control the money and the multinational corporations, thus acting as a shadow government which pulls the strings that affect every human on earth. They try to manipulate the "kings" who sit in political seats of power. Often the "kings" of politics despise the "captains" of finance, but can do little against them.

The "captains" control so much money and so much production of needed services and goods that the governments are often powerless to do more than enact lip-action against them. But the "captains" can do more than lip-control the "kings." He who holds the purse holds the final power and wields the biggest stick in world affairs.

Some multinational corporations are bigger than some countries they are in, financially speaking.

It is not that the "kings" want to acquiesce to the "captains of world power"—it is that they are **forced** to, as previously indicated.

Chapter

4

The Shocking Nearness of the Depression

The international monetary hurricane swirling over Europe and North America has economists pessimistic and politicians bewildered as to what to do.

The biggest problem of all is the monetization of the federal debt by the Federal Reserve System. The Federal Reserve has to monetize (finance) federal government debt. In the 1950's the debt was around 25 billion dollars. Now it is well over 100 billion dollars, with a staggering amount of interest to be paid by taxpayers to the Federal Reserve owners who hold the government's bonds in lieu of the loan to finance government expenditures.

Yet Mr. Miller, the new Chairman of the Federal Reserve Board is in an accommodating mood as far as the President is concerned. Virtually what the President wants from the Fed he gets! This hurts, especially if there is an inexperienced President who has never spent time in Washington's circles prior to his election, who has little background knowledge and experience of how the system works. How easy it is to spend money when all you have to do is sell more bonds to the men who run the presses, and then let the debt mount up! The taxpayers of another generation will pay it. In the meantime the President can afford to look like Mr. Good Guy all the way! He and the Congress can spend and spend, but we are the ones to get it in the neck with the declining purchasing power of the dollar.

From 1974 to the present, the dollar has lost 54 percent of its purchasing power, primarily because of government-initiated overprinting of paper money.

Since 1967 the dollar has lost over 91 percent of its purchasing power; now we have only 9 cents left in purchasing power of the 1967 dollar! Who is to blame? Those who print the dollars so plentifully, making them worth less and less and less on the world market. Ten to 20 percent annual pay raises still produce deficits at the end of 12 to 24 months for you, as inflation eats up the raises. Include extra taxation on the new income, and you are really in the hole!

About 60 percent of all paper money is in the form of one-dollar bills. They are printed on high-speed rotary presses that operate 24 hours a day! A single rotary press can print one side of 1280 dollar bills in one minute.

ALARMING WARNING BY THOSE IN THE KNOW— "The nation is headed toward a depression worse than that of 1929 because of federal government overspending and rising interest rates," a veteran White House economic advisor warned. Speaking at a mid-year economic outlook seminar at Flagstaff (Arizona) Albert E. Sindlinger, president of Sinlinger and Company Marketing and Opinion Research, said that while most economists are debating the 50-50 odds on recession, "the one thing I'm concerned about is the 50-50 odds on depression" (**Daily News Digest**, August 2, 1978).

"We look for a weaker dollar, runaway prices, inflation, higher interest rates, a severe credit crunch, a depression in 1979, and a stock market crash!" (**International Investor's Viewpoint**, July, 1978).

"Inflation is rising sharply, not only in the U.S. but worldwide, due to the fall in the dollar and its effect on international values. Slowly but surely the wealth built up by generations of prudent Westerners is being frittered away. Even worse, as the inflation rates rise, recession worldwide shows all signs of slowly strangling the economic growth of the whole world. The outlook is bleak and we remain extremely pessimistic about the whole world political-economic picture at the present time. There will be a continued fall in the dollar. What we are seeing is just a trickle! Next could come a wash and finally the horror of a deluge" (Alex Herbage, IMAC Commodities, New York City, June, 1978).

Tim Holt of the Holt Investment Advisory (New York City) says, "The economy is really standing on shaky ground and the stock market will collapse during the weeks ahead. The approaching worldwide depression will generate increasing demand for gold" (June, 1978).

R.E. McMaster of the **Reaper** (July, 1978) said, "I would view the international economic situation as being in the worst of crisis."

Howard Ruff of the **Ruff Times** (July, 1978) says, "The runaway growth of the demands of the people upon our government to give them what they want or think they need is causing us to lose our freedom and is leading us into bankruptcy. I would not be surprised to see a Federal budget of $800 billion within two years with monstrous deficits and runaway inflation. It is politically irreversible. Not enough people want to change. There will be civil chaos in our big cities and periodic interruptions in the delivery of goods and services. One is foolish if he doesn't make plans to relocate or prepare himself with the basic necessities of life to enable him to get through the difficult period ahead."

The Investment Outlook (May, 1978) says, "Typically consumers overextend themselves financially by incurring large debts to buy major appliances, autos, and homes. In the past, when the amount of overall net installments extensions has reached 2 percent of personal income, the economy has subsequently gone into a recession. That ratio now stands at about 2 percent."

Ruff again says, "The U.S. is firmly on the same road to inflationary ruin trod by other civilizations. We face accelerating inflation, eventual hyper-inflation, distrust of all paper currencies, and eventual deflationary collapse followed by a long depression. Get some stored food, gold and silver coins, and homes in a small town, a supply of greenbacks on hand, and an alternate source of heat."

Economist Eliot Janeway says, "America is approaching a depression that could make the slump of the thirties seem like a Tea Party" (Daily News Digest, July, 1978).

Economist Vern Myers says, "There is no precedent in world history for what we face today. We are facing the collapse of the currency of the world—and thus the collapse of the world monetary system. Somewhere along the road, **we are bound to get a rush on the banks.** No, what you are looking at is not a depression, **it is the destruction of the social order, the end of our era. It will be triggered by the collapse of this inflation"** (Daily News Digest, January, 1978).

Alvin Toffler, author of **Future Shock** (May, 1976) said, "The world is at a critical juncture. We are on the brink of another revolution. Today's economic recession is just a taste of what is to come. Our economic system is in danger of collapse . . . not just in the U.S., but around the world."

The OPEC nations have just announced another oil price hike for the 1978-79 era of at least 10 percent. The big threat from them is that they may dump the dollar in place of the new ideas coming out of Europe for a new type of money, or they may use the "basket of currencies" presently being utilized in Europe until ECU gets on the market.

When the oil nations dump the dollar, it will hurt internationally, and **no one in the power circles of the U.S. knows how badly we will be hurt.**

It could bring about widespread international monetary panic. Non-oil nations who hold many dollars may (like the oil nations) dump them immediately on the international money market and depress the value so far that a complete depression will result. Their dumping would be a panic act on behalf of their own financial security. To hold billions of American dollars after the OPEC nations dump it could be disastrous for both them and us. If they dump, we are done! Even if they hold our dollars, awaiting action from Washington to stabilize the dying dollar, what can be done? Our gold is being auctioned off like it was nothing! The stock market will virtually slide into a depression itself!

We are in for serious depressionary consequences if the OPEC nations dump the dollar in 1979.

We have another Arab problem. If they decide to join the militant forces against President Sadat of Egypt, in opposition to what the U.S. accomplished at the Camp David Israeli-Egyptian accords, **they could cut off our oil supply in an Arab oil embargo.**

That could bring not only consideration of an immediate U.S. attack on the Middle East, but it could also bring a depression to this country such as we have never seen before.

It is not that we do not produce our own oil, nor that we do not have reserves of oil. But the very psychology of the embargo would depress the stock market and throw manufacturers into a psychological tailspin because they wouldn't know where they were going or how much they could produce in the near or distant future. **Mass layoffs would result. There would be panic buying on the part of the immediate gas rationing. Resort areas would become disaster areas. Real estate building would come to a standstill, as would virtually all production in the country.**

If war was considered and entered into, all oil and related energy supplies would be gobbled up by the government to support the military machinery needed to open the oil fields again.

I can see the Soviet Union drawn into the fray immediately, on behalf of the PLO and militant Arab oil nations. The Soviets want to please the Arabs in order to get their oil, and they would like nothing better than to see the Western flow of oil terminated and the mighty American Empire crippled.

An Arab oil embargo or the dumping of the dollar for another monetary system could put us into a depression and war overnight!

Throughout the country, the number one problem people are talking about is not the Egyptian-Israeli accord or consequent problems stemming from PLO resentment or fiery statements.

It is not that we need to cut back on oil-energy consumption. If properly presented with a definite plan of action, Americans have the ability and love for their country and way of life, to comply. We are not babies who have to have our sucker, as some have stated. There would not be mass rejection of a reduction in uses of energy.

The number one topic in discussions everywhere today is government spending, resulting in higher and higher taxes, and the ridiculousness of many of the government-supported and financed programs.

Consider what Representative Philip Crane (R-Illinois, Daily News Digest, June, 1978) had to say about taxes. "Taxes of the federal and local governments are gobbling up 45 percent of our national income. At the turn of the century, government at all levels in this country was taking 3 percent of the national income. That increased to 13 percent in 1929, with ⅓ federal taxes and ⅔ state taxes, and now presently 45 percent, of which ⅓ is state and local, and the federal take is ⅔." Crane went on to say that he fears we are going in the dangerous direction of Great Britain, which now takes 60 percent of the national income in taxes. This results in a lack of capital in the private business sector and a squeeze of investments, resulting in loss of jobs and of real growth in the economy. The nation's annual productivity is hovering at 3.3 percent while U.S. major trading partners, West Germany and Japan, are at 5.8 percent and 10.3 percent, respectively," Crane reported. I can only add that West Germany and Japan are among the world's highest users of imported oil, along with the leader, the United States. West Germany has one of the lowest rates of inflation in the Western world today, and yet is a great industrial nation, using much energy. But she has leaders exercising fiscal and monetary restraint rather than enjoying the euphoria of engaging in cosmetic programs to please the people and/or other nations for political reasons. The Germans drastically cut the government's enlarged budget and removed all wage and price controls. They also cut many social welfare spending programs. Within one year inflation was stopped, the German mark had become an internationally recognized "hard currency," and its economy took on a prosperous expansion which is continuing today with less than 2 percent inflation annually!

If they did it through cutting of government expenditures "against the counsel of the Americans," even though it meant a terribly unpopular move at the time, we can too.

Depression can be stopped, as indicated in an article appearing in Johnny Johnson's **Daily News Digest** attributing the origin of the story to Vermont Royster in a feature article in the **Wall Street Journal** of May 10, 1978.

> In 1958, France was in political turmoil. The Indochina war had been lost, the country was near civil war over Algeria, and the economy was wracked by inflation. TO BUY A PAIR OF SHOES YOU COUNTED OUT FRANCS BY THE THOUSANDS. In desperation the country looked to de Gaulle. The general was no economist, but he did understand that if France was to be restored to "glory" it required restoration of the French franc. In his memoirs he tells how Jacques Rueff persuaded him against the advice of his political staff (INCLUDING SOME IN THE BANK OF FRANCE) to accept officially the devaluation of the old franc, that in fact had already happened, to chop zeros off the old franc and issue new ones, and to match that with sharp reductions in the SUBSIDIES TO NATIONAL INDUSTRIES AND OTHER BUDGET ITEMS.
>
> In the next three years France saw a sharp drop in both the rate of inflation and the unemployment, an end to its balance-of-payments problems, and an increase in both industrial and agricultural production!

Now look at America by comparison. President Truman's last budget called for government expenditures of 78.6 billion dollars, with a deficit of 9.9 billion dollars. President Eisenhower's first budget cut expenditures to 67.5 billion dollars and the deficit to 3 billion. We now have a budget of over 500 billion dollars, with a conceded deficit of at least 60 billion dollars, as stated by the President!

We have not grown that much in population from Eisenhower till now to justify this budget. Why all the inflationary programs of today and not then? This budget will produce a great depression. We can stop it with our President announcing a 60-billion-dollar out for 1979, another 50 billion-dollar cut for 1980, and still another substantial cut for 1981. If you do that, Mr. President, you will be our next President and loved by all the people, except the ones who won't get the hand-outs and who will have to go back to work for a living. The President will not be popular at first with some members of Congress who have planned fantastic programs for their constituencies, but even they will love him soon, as the majority of the people in their states will give them partial credit for "falling in step with Prudent President." If they don't, they'll be voted out. There is nothing as popular in this country today as tax reform! Give us a man who will pledge with all his heart to give us taxation relief as President, and show us simply how he is going to do it, and you have the next President of the United States.

Chapter

5

The Incredible Gold Secret

Gold is shooting up in price and value astronomically, from its original 35 dollars per ounce to today's price of well over 225 dollars per ounce.

I know of many people who have my booklets on the subject in the past five years and who have made small fortunes and perhaps larger ones buying gold.

I recommended back in 1974, "Sell your house and buy gold—it will rise in value far faster." I suggested that you sell your stocks and mutual funds, get out of treasury bonds and commodities, and get into gold coins or bullion (not into paper stocks on gold) and hold the gold for as long as you can afford to.

The letters I receive now are most gratifying from some of my followers who have really made it in gold. I am so thrilled for them.

But the gold rush is far from over. I believe we are now just seeing the beginnings of the real gold mine you have in owning gold coins.

As confidence in the dollar continues to go down worldwide, confidence in gold and silver goes up. Gold has always been number one in the minds of the human race as the greatest store of value. It has been so since the days of the Book of Genesis in the Bible and will continue to be until gold is toppled from its supreme role as monetary king just before the Battle of Armageddon (Revelation 18).

It is predicted in the amazing Bible prophecies that God will destroy the commercial systems of the world under the new-world government that will be set up in Europe and carried to its new headquarters in Jerusalem by a world-wide dictator known in some circles as Mr. 666. (The letters incorporated in his name will add up to 666.) Latin, Hebrew, and Greek are the languages having numerical equivalents for letters. It appears that his name will add up to 666 in Greek, but we cannot be positive at this stage of fulfilled prophecy. We'll talk more of this economic dictator later, but suffice it to say that when he takes over the ten nations coming together in Europe in the Common Market, at their invitation (Revelation 17:12), he will take over world gold and silver as quickly as he can in order to support and give backing to his monetary objectives (Daniel 11:42, 43).

Gold has been and will be the greatest store of value for mankind over the long haul.

Other commodities and even blue-chip stocks and real estate possessions may grant short-term and long-term profits, but over the centuries, when all other values have risen and fallen into oblivion forever, gold has held true to its original use—the most valuable material possession a man could have and pass on to his posterity.

Why this strange mystique about gold? Why has gold been a hedge against depression, falling dollars, and hyperinflations?

Gold has held men steady when government-issued flat paper monies rose, fell, and rose again only to fall into permanent destruction. When the flurry of falling monetary systems was over and the governments they torpedoed were gone forever, the new leaders took a fresh look at gold and said, "All along we knew this was what we needed to stabilize our economy!"

Hindsight is so much clearer than foresight!

Gold has strange qualities about it that gather political and economic value to itself. No other kind of money or store of value has ever done this or will ever do this.

Gold has enabled men and families to survive depression when other people who held dollars went into depression and suffered great losses.

Gold has been a hedge against governments changing the values of paper money. Even when governments exchanged their paper money for another kind of money from the printing presses, gold maintained and sustained many responsible wealthy people during the changeover, and they were unaffected.

As inflation eats into the purchasing power of your dollars and makes them worth less and less, gold usually goes up in its value for the possessor, and buys more and more. That is precisely what is happening now in the role of gold in the economic world we live in.

When depression comes (or even severe recession), and real estate prices drop, and values drop in a thousand other items, gold will retain its value. Its purchasing power will be higher, and though it too may dip some in the long term, it will always be valued higher than any other investment or possession.

Because of the short supply of gold today and the constant demand for it by governments wanting to dump dollars and by Arabs desiring gold instead of dollars, when you own gold you increase your value currently as gold rises in price per ounce. But you also ensure yourself of being in the coveted position of being able to become very wealthy when the financial chips are down for other people and the nation in the coming depression.

If this were not true, why are so many people storing gold in lieu of the predicted depression? Why do brokers recommend buying heavily in gold and silver and staying there?

Why are certain stockbrokers (who usually recommend other stocks and mutual funds and so-called blue-chip investments) now highly recommending to their clients, "Buy gold and hold it?"

Faith in the intrinsic power of gold has never waned, even in ancient history. There has always been solid confidence by the public in the value of owning gold and hiding it, or using it cosmetically somehow. Our wives and lady friends have found many ways to literally enjoy the investments in gold jewelry.

A gentleman recently stopped me in one of my monetary seminars in California to let me know that 2½ years ago he took my advice and pulled his savings out of a savings and loan association and bought $5,000 worth of gold coins and stored them safely.

Just recently, because of great illness he was forced to take the coins back to the coin dealer where he bought them. They gave him $25,000 in return for his 2½ year investment; he made 500 percent on his 30-month investment. No wonder he told me he loved me!

Another broker in Newport Beach, California, told me he was steering most of his clients into gold and silver coins for the time being, though his real money had been in real estate. His comments were, "Real estate is priced too high right now and will soon fall terribly. We are going to have a terrible depression in this country and I am advising all my people not to buy stocks, as the market is going to suffer heavy losses and a calamitous crash. After that, they can take their gold coins and silver coins with real innate value and buy houses, land, factories, and utilities at a fraction of the price they are selling for today. Gold will go up, so will silver, and everything else will come down."

He continued: "My daddy bought many houses in Corona del Mar, for a pittance in 1929 and 1930 just because he saw the depression coming, dumped his possessions, bought gold and waited for the rainy day. It came and he became a millionaire overnight, all because of owning a little gold.''

Not a bad story. It can be yours too. Maybe you have no desire to become a millionaire. You just want to live comfortably for the rest of your life. Let me assure you of three things that are certain in our future. There are more things than that (which we'll touch on in the last chapter of this book,) but let's consider three things for now.

First, expect changes every day, every week, every month, and every year you live. Don't get up in the morning and think that things are always going to go unchanged. Things **will** change, sometimes for the better and sometimes for the worse. Things will happen that you do not look for and do not like. This is life. Nothing remains steady forever.

This does not mean that you are pessimistic about life on a daily basis. You are merely adjusting your thinking to the well-known fact that ''changes may come today and I am going to be ready for them.''

This thinking will enable you to adjust more quickly to the changing life processes constantly surrounding you. Brace yourself, and if you are a believer in God, as I am, then trust in Him to give you the ability to adjust, to change and to stand steady in His divine strength through it all. He is in the helping business. ''Cast all your cares upon Him, for He careth for you'' (1 Peter 5:7).

Secondly, remember that some of these changes will be financial ones. Perhaps your changes will be for the better; consider yourself well-off if they are. However, most of us in this world suffer financial setbacks more than we do windfalls of financial good luck.

However, if you suffer financially like the rest of us, remember that if you have some gold coins stored away (and perhaps some silver coins minted up through the year 1964) you can come out on top when your personal depression comes. You may lose your job and your health, as did the gentleman who bought $5,000 worth of coins 2½ years ago. But like him, you too can make your fortune of $25,000 or much more by owning what is going to produce for you now and in the future.

Thirdly, perhaps you are in such a financial position, though you could be hurt in the coming crash, you feel you will survive it all because of having substantial amounts of greenbacks around and investments that will secure you in the coming storm. May I make one suggestion: make things so good for yourself that you could become very wealthy, with vast fortune at your disposal, by buying gold now.

For those of us who are believers in the divine program of God for the world, why not make yourself more comfortable in the coming catastrophic period of tribulation by owning gold now? You will not only be able to eat better then, but you will be able to help your church, your minister, and the program of evangelization far better than if you were broke and depressed yourself. Perhaps God wants to use you in a new way for His plan and His glory.

Governments may try to erase the mystique of gold, economists may try to advise against it, investors may shy away from it, but there is still in the minds of men the one fact that gold is the true store of value. I can trust gold in the monetary world like I can trust God spiritually.

If you own $10,000 worth of gold coins when the crash comes, think of what could happen.

First, prices will fall about 80 to 90 percent across the board in the United States and Canada, and wherever the depression hits internationally.

Millions will be out of work and consequently hardly able to exist without government help in the form of food, etc.

You have $10,000 in gold and silver coins, perhaps equally divided between the two metals.

Food has come down 90 percent in price, as it will. Whereas you once spent $50 on groceries for a week, now you will be spending $5, and no more than $10 if there is an 80 percent drop in pricing. But you have gold too. So while the dollar is almost completely dead and is purchasing little, though prices have fallen, with your silver coins or gold coins (silver for smaller items and gold for larger needs) you go to the store with a couple of coins. You may well find that a South African Krugerrand gold coin that you paid $140 for in 1977, or $230 for in 1978, is now worth about $500 or more on the open market. They have climbed in value because everybody wants them now that the dollar is dead, or nearly dead. Confidence is in gold. Gold's scarcity will contribute to its value. The dollar's death will contribute greatly to gold's increased value.

So, instead of one coin being worth $200 or $250 now, you have doubled or tripled its value at the same time that other prices are falling catastrophically! Your personal store of gold value went from a $10,000 investment to a $25,000 or even a $50,000 store of value overnight!

If prices have dropped only 80 percent from the time you had $10,000 in gold, and your gold did not go up at all (which it definitely will), you have gained at least 80 percent on your money by the fallen prices. But even that would be good news if everyone around you lost their savings, or were wiped out, or were out of employment and had no income. You would be sitting pretty as a result of your prudence, thoughtfulness, and investment in gold.

Instead of your $10,000 making a mere down payment on the home of your choice, **you might be able to buy it free and clear of any encumbrances financially!**

When the depression lessens the value of the dollar and all products, including all real estate, then you are that much to the good by having held your wealth in gold.

The truth of the matter is that you have a phenomenal increase in the immediate value of your possession, while other people have an immediate devaluation of their holdings. You may come out with a small fortune. You may also come out with a **large** fortune of gold to sustain you and help others you love.

For those dedicated followers of Jesus Christ whom I meet through TV and in my seminars from coast to coast, we can support our church, our ministers, and our favorite ministries during this time of tragedy, when many will need the church and its ministries to help them through the toughness of this period. When adversity strikes, many will turn to God, and rightly so. It is one of the good things that happens to the minds and souls of people who normally would not think of Him in their entire life except on Easter, Christmas or a special Jewish holiday. Let's make sure that we, the ones who believe in Christ, keep the doors of our churches open and our ministers preaching during this time, by being cautious now in our investments for them.

Virtually no one will be paying today's prices for products, homes, commodities, articles, cars, etc. when the crash comes. All contracts negotiated before the crash will be repriced and renegotiated in light of new interest rates and prices acceptable to the consumer during the crash.

For instance, let's assume you own a car, or that you are paying it off to the bank at a fixed amount of $200 per month for another 20 months when the crash hits America.

Cars just like yours, for which you are paying $200 a

month, will be sold at perhaps 20 percent of today's value. Payments will be $30 to $40 per month on a new transaction for the same car which cost you $8,000 in today's world!

So you have this same car, slightly used and partly paid for, but now you walk in to the bank manager and tell him that like hundreds of thousands of other persons financially crippled in this society of depressed Americans, he can have his car back. You cannot or will not afford the price, because you can go right across the street **with gold coins** and buy the same $8,000 car for $2,000 cash or with phenomenally low payments.

Will he dicker and deal in your direction? Wouldn't you, if you were the bank manager and you were going to have hundreds of cars dumped in your lap? Yes, he will change the whole contract to an acceptable level of financing for you.

In the case of a house, as mentioned before, you will be able to go to the lender who loaned you the money for the mortgage, and perhaps even be able to negotiate a moratorium on the complete payment of the principal and interest for a year or more if you can just arrange to keep the house up, live in it, maintain its painting, plumbing, electrical necessities, and pay the reduced taxes. Yes, the government will reduce your taxes tremendously, commensurate with the degree of the depression.

What is true of houses, cars, and food will be true of all things, perhaps with the exception of gold itself.

If you hold any amount of gold coins (or bullion, though this is unmanageable for most people) **you can buy what you need, eat what you desire, help your local church and ministry, and even become a millionaire in the holdings you will acquire.**

I hear some Christians saying now (some of them certainly not all, thank God), "Don't you know the Bible says not to lay up for yourselves treasures on earth, but to lay them up in heaven? Don't you know that Jesus taught us not to think about what we are going to eat and drink or what we will be clothed with, but to seek Him first and all these other things will be added unto us?"

Yes, I am quite aware of both teachings. But let us take them in their own setting, for a text taken out of context becomes a pretext!

When Jesus taught us not to lay up for ourselves treasures on earth, he was teaching against putting our faith in monetary treasures and in things on earth. We are not to put our faith in "things" or "accomplishments" or earthly "treasures" **that crowd out Christ and Christianity. He was warning against evil, Satanic substitutes for real salvation.** Never did he say that it is evil to have money or things. It is not **money** that is the root of all evil; it is **the love of money** that is the root of all evil, said Paul in First Timothy 6:10.

This is what Christ was warning against.

In order to lay up some treasures above for Christ and the cause of His kingdom, it would certainly help matters if you had some money, some gold, with which to do so, when the chaos comes and no one else in your church can help!

When Jesus taught, "Seek ye first the kingdom and His righteousness, and all these things shall be added unto you," He was teaching **Put God first; Put salvation first.** Then God will add the necessities of life to you in the normal course of living or even more dramatically if He chooses. The fact that God allows many Christians to have money is a fulfillment of Matthew 6:32, 33. He is already adding these blessings to those who have put Him first. There are many wealthy Christians who support the works of God today, both at home and abroad. There are many "average-income Christians" who support the world efforts of evangelizing, as they too are enjoying "God adding it to them daily."

If you are a Christian and are enjoying a good job and good security, and you could save more than you do, and you **could buy** some gold coins instead of spending everything you earn on pleasure, etc., then who is to blame when the crash comes, and you come up broke like everybody else?

"He becometh poor that dealeth with a slack hand, but the hand of the diligent maketh rich" (Proverbs 10:4).

"He that gathereth in summer is a wise son, but he that sleepeth in harvest is a son that causeth shame" (Proverbs 10:5).

For the love of money is the root of all evil: which while some coveted after, they have erred from the faith, and pierced themselves through with many sorrows" (1 Timothy 6:10).

"Honor the Lord with thy substance, and with the first fruits of all thine increase: So shall thy barns be filled with plenty, and thy presses shall burst out with new wine" (Proverbs 3:9, 10).

Why would the Arabs rather have gold than greenbacks in payment for their oil? Why are so many superrich and not-so-rich investors dropping their varied stock portfolios and buying gold? Why is the American government even bothering to sell gold to redeem the falling dollar? The answer to all of these questions is that gold is valuable to have, to hold, and to negotiate with when the chips are down. And the chips are now down for the dollar. The government is using the greatest negotiable asset they have to help it.

This should tell us something about the value of gold itself. What is gold anyway?

1. Gold is more than a source of raw commercial

power. It has also been one of the most consistent and aggressive civilizing forces ever known to man. The history of gold is actually the history of civilization. Many occurrences of greed, brutality, and warfare have accompanied the quest for gold. But the lust for gold also has brought mankind enormous benefits. God seems to have ordained gold to be the foremost metal of the arts, the world's most effective and useful money, and an industrial commodity of incomparable value. It was even said as early as Genesis 2:12, "And the gold of that land is good; there is bdellium and the onyx stone." Gold was valued in the second chapter of the book of man's history!

2. Gold is a dense (19.3 times heavier than water), soft, bright, yellow metal of rare beauty. It is the most imperishable and stable of the metallic elements. It is immune to the effects of weather and oxygen. It does not tarnish, rust, or corrode. It holds up against most acids and alkalis and survives immersion in saltwater or freshwater indefinitely without change. It is also the most easily worked and fabricated of all the metals.

3. Gold is seldom used in its pure state because of its softness, but is combined with another metal (an alloy) to make it harder. The purity of gold is measured in carats: pure gold is 24 carats fine. Gold was used extensively throughout Solomon's Temple as the chief metal to glorify the God of Israel. When the Israelites wanted to offer God the best, they gave Him gold!

4. Gold occurs in nature as free or pure gold, or else in combination with other minerals. Free gold (dust, grains, or nuggets) is recovered from sand or gravel by placer mining (the sand or gravel is agitated in water and the gold settles to the bottom). When the free gold is found in veins or lodes, the rock bearing the metal is mined and crushed. Ore containing gold in combination

with other metals must first be crushed fine, after which the gold is extracted by chemical processes.

5. It was the lust for gold that motivated early Spanish adventurers in the twin Americas. They found it abundantly in Peru and Bolivia, and carried vast fortunes back to enrich their homeland; other South American areas made lesser contributions. In Europe prior to 1890 the chief source of gold was the Ural Mountains of Russia. When gold was discovered in California in 1848, the U.S. soon took the world lead in production and held it for about 70 years. But then a gold field in Rhodesia and the Transvaal (South Africa) forged ahead and now holds first place among gold-producing regions, with a yearly output that in normal years is more than half of the whole world's production. The supply there seems to be unlimited!

Is it any wonder that the Soviet Union enjoys the U.S. working against its own best interests in South Africa by fighting the white government there over the apartheid problem? We may succeed in dumping South Africa from the U.N. and get most of the world to dump its relationships with this gold-producing area.

When we turn our back on this Western government of democratic principles, we lose gold to the Soviets eventually, who could take it over, using black, Marxist guerrillas to overthrow the government. There are Cuban instructors in many places in Africa to train African guerrillas to overthrow white regimes: Canadian-French forces from Quebec are now being trained in Cuba to terrorize the rest of Canada and to reach into the United States.

6. The gold standard is a monetary system in which all forms of legal tender may be converted on demand into fixed quantities of fine gold as defined by law. Until the nineteenth century, most countries of the world maintained a bimetallic monetary system (a double

metallic standard, gold and silver, for coins and currency). The widespread adoption of the gold standard during the second half of the nineteenth century was largely a result of the industrial revolution, which brought about a vast increase in the production of goods, and widened the basis for world trade. The countries which adopted the gold standard were motivated by three principle aims:

A. To facilitate the settlement of international commercial and financial transactions.

B. To establish stability in international exchange rates. (Gold has always been our best store of financial value.)

C. To maintain domestic monetary stability.

7. Gold has been the only commodity to ever acquire a universal acceptance as the best money. Silver has been its rival for centuries, and even copper has played a historical part in the development of money. But through the span of history, gold wins overall.

8. Gold derives its worldwide acceptance and value because almost all men consider it to be the highest form of luxury, and human demands for luxuries are endless. Gold is portable, homogenous, and readily divided into small portions with each having a high unit value. Gold is the ideal commodity money.

God told the children of Israel in Egyptian bondage what to do before they left Egypt in Moses' day: "And the children of Israel did according to the word of Moses; and they borrowed of the Egyptians jewels of silver, and jewels of gold, and raiment" (Exodus 12:35).

9. Most modern economic theory tends to deny the need of a commodity basis for money. (Strange that it has worked so well for centuries! Guess we just know so much more today!) The Keynesian Theory, (by John Maynard Keynes, a British economist from 1883 to

1946) holds that any link of any commodity (such as gold) with money places unnecessary and often dangerous restrictions on the government's ability to manage the national economy.

(Wow,did he say it right! That is exactly what led this present government for the past ten years to demonetize gold from our dollar! And look where it got the U.S.A.—it certainly lifted printing restrictions on the dollar!)

10. Any past attempt to base money on intangibles only (as our government is doing now), such as credit, or government edict or fiat, has ended in inflationary panic and disaster. People have no confidence in this money and when people lose faith in the value of their money, they lose faith in the government that issued that currency. History proves this to be true. Why cannot the American government learn this? They know it; they know it well. And those who know it best may well be the very ones producing the very fall of the dollar that we are seeing, as they lead this country into a terrible depression. Then, with a loss of everything, they will force us into the one salvation left—one-world government.

11. Whenever an overall breakdown of a monetary system occurs, a return to gold always restores order, revives confidence, and brings back prosperity. This is why I have often used the phrase in my seminars, **"Gold is God's secret power for believers and the church to be maintained in the tribulation days ahead."**

Gold was one of the first metals noticed by man. It was also the first element and substance to be mentioned in the Bible, and the last monetary element to be crushed in the Book of Revelation. God meant for us to use it wisely.

And a river went out of Eden to water the garden; and from thence it was parted, and became into four heads. The name of the first is Pison; that is it which compasseth the whole land of Havilah, where there is gold; and the gold of that land is good (Genesis 2:10-12).

Therefore shall all her (earth's) plagues come in one day, death and mourning and famine; and she shall be utterly burned with fire . . . And the merchants of the earth shall weep and mourn over her; for no man buyeth their merchandise anymore: The merchandise of gold and silver and precious stones and pearls . . . (Revelation 18:8, 11, 12).

12. The hoarding or keeping of gold during economic strife becomes more and more intense. That is why the price of gold rises at the slightest indication of economic, political, or military problems. But after the trouble passes, the gold usually comes back into circulation.

13. China used gold to expedite its huge wheat purchase from Canada, in 1970 (98 million bushels). Gold is still the world's most acceptable international money. Without it, Red China would have either faced mass starvation or been forced to appeal to the Western powers for credit.

14. The demonetization of gold started the beginning of every known inflation in the past. Since 1968, when the legal requirement for a 25 percent backing of Federal Reserve currency was done away with, the United States has had no contact between its money system and gold. On August 15, 1971, the right of foreign central banks to convert their surplus dollars into gold was suspended.

15. Gold coins offer the most excellent way to preserve capital in inflationary times. They also have the advantage of being easily hidden.

16. During the 60's, the United States lost more than half of its gold reserves, and at the same time accumulated more debts than had ever previously existed as a nation for 184 years!

17. Gold will not be replaced in the near future. It is the world's most effective and trusted store of value; it is the ideal money. If gold remains the "essential yet undeclared world money," then an eruptive rise in its price is unavoidable. Also, a dramatic change in the price of gold is bound to have drastic social and political effects as well as financial and economic effects. This is happening right now as gold rises higher and higher every month.

18. There are three ways a nation may obtain gold: mine it, earn it through balance-of-payments surpluses, or bid for it on the open market.

19. There was a time when most nations felt that the U.S. would have enough gold to cover its international debts by mining it, buying it, and securing it through trade. This is no longer so, and the nations fear debt with the U.S.A. They do not like our method of payment—dollars. Dollars are dying, and therefore the world is suffering from acute financial indigestion.

20. The amount of gold which the Russians have sold to the West over the past two decades lets us know they have a great need to trade with the West. It also shows us that the Soviet Union is probably the second-ranking gold producer, second only to South Africa (which someday she could control as well).

21. The Communists need gold just as much as any nation. Despite their propaganda, they know that no

foreigner in his right mind would accept Russian rubles in payment. At present the U.S. dollar is a shaky currency, but in comparison to the Russian ruble it is a mountain of strength. Soviet currency is so unreliable and inflation has risen so much that the Soviet people abhor the ruble. Therefore, gold-smuggling behind the Iron Curtain prevails.

22. Hoarding of gold is evident when the paper money is dying in any nation. According to Dr. Franz Pick, world currency expert, people have already hoarded about 4000 tons of gold here in America. Half of this is stored in foreign banks and half in domestic banks or in private homes. Dr. Pick believes that Americans own about 2 billion dollars of the estimated 25 billion dollars of privately owned gold in the world. That figure is growing all the time as Americans turn to the safe store of value for their savings.

23. Gold does not have the industrial use that silver has, but the demand for commercial gold in recent years has increased at a fantastic rate. The gold-plating of delicate electrical circuits and components as an anticorrosion measure is now commonly performed in electronics, computers, and aerospace technologies. Other scientific and technical uses are also expanding, including the dental, jewelry, and artistic uses which expand with the increasing world population.

24. One last fact to remember: **More people have gold now, and are buying gold now, than ever before in world history. More uses have been introduced and discovered for gold usage than ever before in history. No metal has been found by man in his whole history to take the place of gold, nor do we expect one to be found at this later date.**

Chapter

6

Rush to Your Bank!

The questions pour into me: "When will the crash come? What can I do about my money in the bank or in the savings and loan?" "How can I save my life savings?" "I'll be ruined completely and have to go on welfare. I live off my interest!" "What can we do now?" "What should I do about my real estate holdings?"

Do nothing until you are through reading this book and have checked the facts that I will give you now.

It is true that you should rush to your bank and draw out your savings, **when you see certain things happening in the world.** If you don't, you could lose it all over a long weekend.

If banks fail and go bankrupt for various reasons which we will point out, and if the currency continues to lose its purchasing power as a result of inflation and finally is sold off by the internationalists just before the coming depression, then you will wish you had pulled all your monies out of the savings and loans institutions and banks and put it into something more durable, safe, and long-lasting—something where you can get your hands on it as you need it.

I believe the banks will fail, some through bankruptcies caused by general mismanagement, some as a result of overseas investors pulling the plug, and others by the downdraft of the depression and the resulting runs on the banks.

If about 18 percent of Americans rush to the banks

tomorrow, we will collapse them completely. They could not stand the pressure of such mass withdrawals. They are too loaned out, too badly invested, and too badly managed.

On the following pages you will find a rather complete list of **important events to watch for—signs of an impending crash in the country**. When you see several of these things happening simultaneously, **rush to the bank and save your savings right then.**

1. WATCH FOR BANKRUPT BANKS IN THE NEWS. The Federal Deposit Insurance Corporation recently said that it had 368 banks on its problem list at the end of 1977, down from 379 the year before and a peak of 385 in November, 1975. The FDIC said that among problem banks there were 12 in the "serious problem-virgule-potential payoff" category, down from 24 at the end of 1976. The category includes banks with advanced serious problems and an estimated 50 percent or better of requiring FDIC financial assistance.

Under "serious problem" banks, which threaten to involve the FDIC in a financial outlay unless there is a drastic change, the FDIC listed 100 at the end of 1977, up from 91 the year earlier. Under "other problem" banks, which have serious weaknesses but where the FDIC is less vulnerable, the agency listed 256, down from 264 at the end of 1976.

The FDIC said the list included national and state member banks as well as the nonmember banks it regulates, and that some of the banks on its list are also on problem lists kept by the Federal Reserve Board and the Comptroller of the Currency. Spokesmen for both these bank-regulatory agencies said that neither publishes the total number of problem banks on its list. Do you know whether your bank is on those lists?

The FDIC said that a large number of banks on its problem list were small. It listed 323 banks with deposits of less than $100 million, 31 with deposits of $100 million to $500 million, 7 with deposits of $500 million to $1 billion, and 7 with deposits exceeding $1 billion. **It added that 31 percent of the banks included in the "serious problem-virgule-potential payoff list" since the end of 1973 ultimately failed.** (THAT IS A SERIOUS, ALARMING STATEMENT. GO BACK AND READ IT AGAIN.) The FDIC regulates more than 8500 insured, state-chartered banks that aren't members of the Federal Reserve System. It didn't identify any of the banks on its list. (See the **Wall Street Journal,** March 29, 1978.)

If that sounds ominous to you, and makes you wonder if your bank is on the problem list, ask your bank manager what he knows about it. Ask him to find out for you. Take this report to him and ask him what he knows about his own bank **or the banks he is in competition with in the same community.** Perhaps you need to visit your "across-the-street" bank and ask **that** manager what he knows about **your** bank. You may get a better analysis of your bank through him. If he is honest (and most managers are) he'll tell you the truth, especially if he thinks you might move your account into his bank!

WE HAVE JUST HAD THIS YEAR'S FOURTH BANK FAILURE. Banco Credito & Ahorro Ponceno, Puerto Rico's third-largest bank, was taken over by two other Puerto Rican banks. Banco Credito, the fourth bank to fail this year, was the third-largest bank failure in U.S. history. (See the **Wall Street Journal,** April 3, 1978.)

AN ALABAMA BANK JUST FAILED. Wilcox County Bank of Camden, Alabama, was closed by state authorities on March 3, 1978. The bank had $10.5 billion in deposits and 4300 deposit accounts. The bank was taken over by a new group of local citizens and reopened. (See the **Wall Street Journal,** March 6, 1978.)

A CHICAGO BANK HAD A RUN ON IT BY DEPOSITORS IN CHECKING AND SAVINGS ACCOUNTS. From the **Phoenix Gassette** of January 25, 1978, comes the report that very worried customers withdrew somewhere between $4 billion and $5 billion from savings and checking accounts from the Drovers Bank of Chicago on its first "reopening day," reported John Midigan, vice-president of the newly chartered bank. The Drover's National Bank of Chicago went into receivership and was placed in the hands of the FDIC. It was the first bank failure of 1978 and promises not to be the last in the United States in the 1979-80 period.

There have been four bank failures by the time of this writing this year. We had 6 banks collapse in 1977, 16 in 1976, and 13 in 1975.

"The continued indifference in Washington, evidenced by so little being done to the sliding dollar, which has fallen and is falling to new lows against the German mark and the Swiss franc, could easily plunge the world into a terrible monetary crisis, bankers in America warn. It is extremely hard to get the President's attention to the fate of the dollar at this present time" (**Journal of Commerce**, August 9, 1978).

Bankers in various areas who really understand the national economy and not just the local economy that they are involved with can see the forthcoming tragedy in the American dollar. Many of them are very worried.

SOME BIG BANKS ARE IN TROUBLE WITH OVERSEAS LOANS TO CERTAIN LESSER-DEVELOPED COUNTRIES WHICH ARE UNABLE TO REPAY THEIR LOANS.

The latest news reported by the **Journal of Commerce** (January 17, 1978) is that overseas lending by some of large American banks (involving some great risks for the banking industries involved) is a matter of great concern within Congress. A government report stated that $164 billion or more had gone out of the country to finance ventures overseas, with nearly a quarter of that amount going to very poor countries.

Three federal agencies which regulate U.S. banks made the astonishing report. Most of these countries will not be able to pay even the interest—much less the principal—back to the U.S. banks! Then the banks will pour more money into these countries so they will not have to default on the previous loans!

With this kind of irresponsible loaning from major banking concerns, do you wonder what they are thinking? What if these countries, under Soviet inspiration, simply declare that they cannot pay back anything? Can the banks stand the loss of such billions of dollars? When you read about these things beginning to happen, pull your money out of your bank immediately.

THE BEVERLY HILLS NATIONAL BANK went under in 1973, but you probably didn't read much about it. A run on the bank took place in that prestigious money community!

THE UNITED STATES NATIONAL BANK OF SAN DIEGO folded the same year. Very little was publicized about it.

ONE OF THE LARGEST BANK FAILURES IN AMERICAN HISTORY ALSO WAS REPORTED—THE FRANKLIN NATIONAL BANK OF NEW YORK, with total assets of $3.6 billion. It went completely under.

After that came THE SECURITY NATIONAL BANK OF LONG ISLAND, with assets of over $1.7 billion.

Others you may not have read about in the past three years included the American City National Bank and Trust Company of Milwaukee, the Chidester Bank in Arkansas, the Franklin Bank in Houston, the Northern Ohio Bank, and the Detroit Bank of Commonwealth.

Some of these were bailed out by Arabs with oil money, or by others, but **they all went bankrupt first!**

Overseas, the BANK de FINANLEMENT went bankrupt and was closed by the Swiss government on January 8, 1975.

The HERSTATT BANK, third-largest bank in Germany, also went bankrupt.

The TRIUMPH INVESTMENT TRUST LIMITED IN ENGLAND went bankrupt, along with a list of others.

Representative Henry Reuss (D-Wisconsin), Chairman of the House Banking Committee, warned of the real possibility that U.S. Banks may fail because of heavy losses from speculation in foreign exchange.

Now get this: The Washington Post announced early in 1976 that CHASE MANHATTAN BANK and the NATIONAL CITY BANK, the second and third largest banks in the U.S., were on the Federal list of 150 Problem Banks! These two banks have the highest acclaim and prestige of the nation and the world, **but they are in trouble.** The **Washington Post** indicated that these banks had "a high probability of failure."

Problem banks are those with over 65 percent of their gross capital funds loaned out to shaky situations worldwide.

Many banks are highly criticized for their general mismanagement in every loan department, domestic and foreign, putting them in a very high risk position of failure.

What is happening here in the U.S. has already happened in Australia in this decade. According to the **Los Angeles Times** of October 4, 1974, "The Australian government cut interest rates to ease its credit squeeze after a day of panic when investors rushed to withdraw their savings in Adelaide, Brisbane and Sydney."

Millions of dollars were withdrawn as savers

besieged savings and loan company offices, fearing a deepening crisis for building and land development companies after several recent financial collapses.

Acting Prime Minister Jim Cairns tried to quell the fears at an emergency press conference in the capital, saying that there was "no objective condition" for panic.

Acting Treasurer Bill Hayden announced that the government was reducing interest rates on short-term treasury notes by 1.391 percent, to 9.358 percent, and on longer term notes by 1.283 percent, to 9.472 percent.

He said the cuts would make securities and deposits with banks and financial institutions more attractive.

Cairns said he had conferred with Prime Minister Gough Whitlam in Washington.

He also announced the postponement of his trip to Peking to open an Australian trade exhibition. He avoided linking this with the financial crisis, saying it was because of a misunderstanding over the crew of his Air Force jet not being allowed to wear uniforms.

In Adelaide, South Australia, State Premier Don Dunstan, armed with a loudspeaker, hurried to one savings and loan office to try to placate the crowds, and in Brisbane more than $8 million was reported withdrawn in a few hours.

The labor government came under attack in Parliament, with opposition leader Senator James Webster forecasting "the greatest financial disaster" Australia had known.

Wesley H. Hillendahl, vice-president of the Bank of Hawaii, suggests the early 1980's as the time of economic collapse. (The End of Money, 1975).

What do we mean by collapse? H.A. Merklein defines collapse as a combination of unemployment and inflation so rampant that the market ceases to function effectively. Merklein suggests that, given a 50

percent inflation rate, public confidence in government-issued fiat money tends to break down. Barter
begins to replace the money economy. According to
Merklein's calculations, with a 10 percent unemployment rate, collapse could begin at 30 percent inflation.
This figure was exceeded by the United Kingdom,
Argentina, and Italy when they went under in 1975.
(See **The War on Gold**, by Antony Sutton—an excellent book on gold analysis.)

2. RUSH TO YOUR BANK WHEN YOU HEAR OF ECU READY FOR IMPLEMENTATION IN EUROPE.

The new money, called ECU, is a European Currency
Unit which will be backed by gold and will take the
place of the dollar as the world's reserve currency and
final denominator of world currency, a position held by
the dollar until now.

The potential for this major castastrophe for the
dollar came as President Carter met recently with six
other Western European leaders in Europe to discuss
differences in monetary policy and how to stabilize the
dollar. He gave them such poor assurances regarding
the dollar that they decided arbitarily to produce ECU
and let it take the place of the dollar as the world's
reserve currency if possible, and to make it the final
evaluation of all monies, a position held by the dollar
and only by the dollar in world history. When ECU
takes shape (which could happen anytime within 12
months, as there is a large committee working on it
right now in the Common Market nations), it will dump
the dollar and replace it in world currencies as the
reserve tender. No matter where the dollar is held—in
banks, savings and loans, institutions, governments,
industries, investors, you and me—we will all be hit so
hard by this depreciating monetary hurricane that I'm
not sure who will survive.

ECU will produce an economic tornado when it comes, and the dollar may be virtually wiped away in the minds of some. Do not be in the position of holding many dollars at that time.

A central bank for ECU will be set up, such as the newly proposed European Monetary Fund, which will virtually drop the IMF (International Monetary Fund) which was set up primarily by the U.S. after World War II, to help ailing nations and which is greatly controlled by the U.S. This too will be an action taken against the U.S. dollar by leaders in Europe who are greatly concerned about stabilizing world currencies.

This will also be a step towards one-world money to be imposed later by the great "predicted dictator of Europe," who will produce great socialism, a forced unity of nations, and a final monetary system backed by gold and implemented through a credit card stamped on the back of the right hand (Revelation 13:1-18).

We are getting very close to the Bible's predicted Tribulation period—see Matthew 24:21, 22 and Revelation chapters 6-19.

The **Trilateral Observer** reports that the U.S. is going to have a financial panic which will be "far deeper than the panic of 1907, when credit was not available at any price, and more pervasive than the depression of 1930." This panic will be characterized by a loss of confidence in and a flight out of the U.S. dollar. Sutton feels that this panic is inevitable for the following reasons:

A. Increasingly large federal budget deficits are financed through price inflation. This is what is happening now, and is increasing.

B. There is a mountain of state, city, and unfunded private debt. (As they spend without proper income, having to borrow through bonds, etc., it will lead to many New York cities, except worse. How can the government bail them all out?)

   C. Enormous debts are owed to foreign sources.

   D. The U.S. does not have much good (999) gold.

   E. The U.S. is still embarked on its fiat-money, anti-gold crusade, stifling its Western friends and subsidizing its marxist enemies, while by contrast the major European governments, led by West Germany and France, are moving with extraordinary and unparalleled rapidity to protect Europe from the coming financial holocaust by planning for the new European currency (ECU), which will be gold-based and in circulation within five years! Sutton feels that the U.S. dollar will lose when challenged by this new gold-based system. He says that members of the Trilateral Commission, set up by David Rockefeller, are largely responsible for bringing about the ultimate fall of the dollar, the timing of which cannot be accurately forecast. He does not feel that this will happen during the next 12-24 months. Those who are self-sufficient and have taken precautionary moves will weather the coming panic. Those who depend on the government will lose. (Sutton believes heavily in owning gold. See the **Daily News Digest**, September 20, 1978).

3. RUSH TO YOUR BANK WHEN YOU SEE THE STOCK MARKET SLIPPING OVER A HUNDRED POINTS IN ONE WEEK.

   When Wall Street, which is the banking and investment center of the U.S. feels international and domestic financial jitters, you will know it in the price of stocks as they fall, and when the word in New York is "sell!"

   You can get the Stock Market report daily on some radio stations and in most newspapers. The ups and downs of the market are everyday occurrences, but when the market slips downward consistently and then all of a sudden you realize it is close to 700 or 600 or even 500 points of the Dow Jones average daily, you should have sold out a year ago, when things were high and fairly prosperous. But at least now, RUSH TO YOUR BANK AND DRAW OUT WHAT YOU HAVE THERE AND CONVERT THOSE DOLLARS TO GOLD AND SILVER COINS FAST, NO MATTER WHAT YOU LOSE IN INTEREST IN THE BANK OR WHAT THE GOLD OR SILVER COSTS.

The Stock Market hurricane will catch the value of the dollar, and they will both fall into the ditch. But you needn't follow them to bankruptcy if you are prudent, watchful and prompt.

4. WHEN EMERGENCY LEGISLATION IS PASSED BY THE GOVERNMENT TO LIMIT INFLATIONARY SPIRALS BY IMPOSING STIFFER AND STIFFER WAGE AND PRICE CONTROLS, RUSH TO YOUR BANK.

Often, when a government is spending too much money and causing the money supply to increase tremendously, as in today's situation, the government imposes sudden wage and price controls after suggesting that prices be controlled by personal incentive rather than legislatively. This means that we will have ceilings that make the marketplace of the nation immediately depressed. Wage and price controls do not help.

This is one way the government has of "placing the blame on business." But when the controls are enacted, the marketplace loses its incentive to produce products and manufacture goods. Unemployment increases as companies rely more on built-up inventories than on new productions. That means raw material purchases are down, welfare rolls are increased and unemployment insurance is drained by those who are idled by the mass layoffs. Recession sets in if this trend is continued. This kind of control is what Washington is considering now. It is patchwork economics; it is like placing a Band-Aid on a cancer, when immediate surgery is required to cut out the cancer. But if the surgery is too painful for the politicians, if it costs them too much loss in popularity, then they engage in patchwork economics, placing the blame here and there instead of on enormous spending.

5. RUSH TO YOUR BANK WHEN YOU HEAR THAT UNEMPLOYMENT IS NEARING 10 or 11 PERCENT.

With this kind of unemployment in the U.S. or Canada, less money will be in circulation throughout the country on every level of life and business. The general marketplace of business will be down tragically, for when there is less money circulating, there is less buying and selling, less producing and manufacturing, and suddenly the mood of gloom is so pervasive in the nation that depression hits overnight.

Government unemployment statistics do not always tell the whole story. Dropped from the statistics are those people who have given up trying to find a job after trying for a long time. There are cities in the U.S. that already have 9 or 10 percent unemployment. If the government ever admits 9 percent, then rest assured it is at least 11 percent! Rush to your bank. Do not lose your savings!

6. RUSH TO YOUR BANK WHEN YOU DISCOVER THAT IT HAS FAR MORE FOREIGN DEPOSITORS THAN DOMESTIC.

If your bank is primarily funded by overseas investors and depositors, then it stands a good chance of losing its capital on the whims of those overseas depositors. For example, in the changing Arab world of alliances and political hatreds (currently being built up by the PLO against President Carter, President Sadat, and Prime Minister Begin over the recent Camp David peace accords), any one of the Arab nations which has great investments in that bank could easily retaliate by withdrawing everything they have in the bank.

If the bank has been using these funds to loan out money to borrowers (as they all do), making money on money in the form of interest, what happens if the money is withdrawn? What happens to that bank if the withdrawal is requested and the money is not there? Believe me, that will be the case soon. That bank could fold overnight, as have several others in the 70's. Not only the investors, but many depositors could go down the drain with that bankrupt bank.

7. RUSH TO YOUR BANK IF AND WHEN YOU NOTICE GOLD AND SILVER RISING IN PRICE ASTRONOMICALLY ON THE WORLD MARKET.

It is very difficult for most of the nation's hardworking people to know what is happening in all the markets of the world when it comes to weekly money values. But one prime indicator that something is tragically wrong with our dollar is when gold rises quickly on a day-by-day basis. This is telling you that something is happening in the money markets of the world. Gold rises overnight when large losses of confidence in the dollar appear. And remember that a lot of this is "mob psychology" on Wall Street. It is a psychology to be aware of, and then get going to your bank. Draw out all you can and buy gold. Do not be left holding thousands in dollars that are dying.

8. RUSH TO YOUR BANK WHEN THE ARAB OPEC NATIONS FINALLY DECIDE TO DUMP THE DOLLAR

AS PAYMENT FOR OIL PURCHASES.

They will. They are talking about it every day now. They are meeting again to raise the price of oil because of the declining dollar. Along with bitterness over the Israeli-Egyptian peace accords being finalized, they hate the constant depreciation of the U.S. dollar and want to get into a more stable currency for the payment of oil. If they select gold only, gold would leap in value to heights unseen! But that seems unlikely, for I don't believe there is enough gold available for that move. However, I could be wrong on that score, so watch for the possibility of the Arabs turning to all-gold currency.

If gold were selected, most nations would be in trouble, and especially the U.S., since we are auctioning off our gold to support the dollar. This process is considered by many people to be idiotic, and I agree. In the event of a gold standard, we would not have anything to buy oil with! Many other nations would be in the same plight.

The Arabs will no doubt accept ECU when it comes out. In the meantime, whatever monetary system they turn to (away from the dollar), it will be catastrophic for the dollar, for Americans, and for you. The psychological implications and ramifications would be overwhelming to the stock market, to money managers, and to the world. Watch for when the Arabs switch. Get to your bank early that day! Beat the rush.

9. RUSH TO YOUR BANK WHEN YOU HEAR OF THE POSSIBILITY OF A "LIMITED WAR" FROM THE SO-VIET UNION UPON AMERICA.

Limited war has been discussed by the Internationalists to force the United States to knuckle under and join the one-world government. It is an alternate route to force us.

Limited war with Russia would mean that they have the opportunity (agreed upon by the power brokers planning the one-world government) to bomb parts of American soil, but not the food areas, wheat belts, etc. This would mean death to millions of Americans in highly populated, dense areas of urban sprawl, and would be intended to stifle domestic initiative towards self-government, thereby killing the will of Americans to resist the plans for joining the country to the one-world government. The limited war would be planned by the superrich, the multinationals who would be safely out of the country. It would be intended to push us into the new government in Europe, set up for "the good of all mankind."

Hopefully this will not happen. However, it might be threatened, and through intimidation alone we could have our people and government acquiesce quietly to the World-union demands.

Is this why so many of the men closest to the President, who sit on the councils mentioned earlier in this book, keep watering down our military position through programs which cut back our ability both to attack first and to defend ourselves? Why do we have so many "doves" next to the President? Why doesn't someone stand up for the defense of America and for a strong strike-first capability when necessary? And, while we are asking, why detente, which builds the enemies and lessens our ability to conquer them if we should be attacked by them? Why SALT, which always weakens us and strengthens them?

Are we headed for the big threat, the day when the final ultimatum comes from the Soviets—that overhead are killer satellites aimed at every city in America, and that we must surrender or be annihilated within five minutes?

Will the next war be fought from outer space, without land forces?.

10. RUSH TO YOUR BANK WHEN THE NONGOVERNMENT ECONOMIC ADVISORS FROM ALL OVER THE NATION SPELL IT OUT LOUD AND CLEAR, SUCH AS THEY ARE DOING NOW!

It is certainly strange how private and government economists disagree on what is happening, and how to cure it. Government economists, controlled by the government interests and their own self-interests, rarely present the real picture of economics. Their statistics are a different set from the private sector of the public economy watchdogs. They juggle, mix, rearrange, take the average, speculate, and predict in such a way that it looks like government is doing fairly well at managing what is obviously a very bad monetary situation. They play down what our neighbors overseas have to say about our dollar. They never say what foreign holders of dollars can do about our dollar should they become totally disenchanted with our government's measures to strengthen the dollar. We are never told the whole story.

I like the writers of private financial letters, advisory letters, and financial reports that are appearing across the nation. These men take daily readings of the economic weather and let you know point-blank what they see and what they recommend. Pay attention to them, especially when they are all saying the same thing, independent of one another, as they are now. (Taken from the Daily News Digest, January—August, 1978):

1. PAT WOOD in **The International August Review:** "Move everything you have into gold and

silver. Now! Don't keep excess cash in dollars or bank accounts. Switch into hard assets. It seems to me to be a perfect time to start buying gold and silver coins again."

2. LAWRENCE HEIM in the **Heim Investment Letter:** He says he was forced back to gold because the U.S. dollar is rotting, is unstable and unpredictable.

3. R.E. McMASTER in **The Reaper:** "We have a major red flag for the economy. An interest rate inversion is underway. That means short-term rates are rising above long-term rates. Such a situation almost always heralds an economic downturn."

4. RICHARD RUSSEL in **Dow Theory Letters:** He expects the Dow to go to new lows and provide "some of the grimmest and most viscious stock-market action yet seen in this entire bear market." The factors bringing about this stock-market collapse will be "massive dividend cuts, bank failures, monetary chaos and collapse of the dollar on an unprecedented scale."

5. **The Robbins Report:** "A financial collapse of all monies is in the making. It will be worse than in the 30's. The third-world countries will default on their debts, and the U.S. and world banks will be in serious trouble. Gold will rise to $300.00 per oz. and silver to $20.00 by 1980. Real estate in small towns best bet now."

6. JOHNNY JOHNSON in the **Daily News Digest:** "The most notable problem is the dollar crisis. That unbacked piece of paper, upon which the entire world has pegged its monetary system, is rapidly losing its credibility. Never before in the recorded history of mankind has a single unbacked currency served as the base for a

world monetary system. If the dollar goes down the tubes, so will the existing monetary systems of the world! Currency problems always lead to social problems. Since the current crisis is worldwide, isn't it safe to assume that a dollar collapse will lead to worldwide social problems?''

7. TOM HOLT in the **Holt Executive Advisory:** "A protracted depression is what investors should anticipate. The stock market is a ticking time bomb and could tumble 350-400 points when this bomb goes off.''

8. VERN MYERS of **Myers Finance & Energy:** "The near-record price of gold is a screaming signal that the money in the world is getting close to the cliff. If gold reaches levels of between $200 and $250 by mid-year, I believe we can expect the financial worldwide panic before the calendar closes.''

(As I write these lines gold is selling at $241.00 per ounce!) It has been said, "He who hesitates 'loses.' '' I hope this will not be your sad story months from now.

Chapter

7

Silver and
the Coming Crash

Gold has always been number one, but silver has always been number two, and definitely deserves a high position in financial recommendations to take you through the coming period of tragedy in the world.

There are those who recommend that in the coming crash you be in three positions financially.

1. Dollar bills at home in your possession, to use for food, etc.

2. Silver coins minted up to and including the year 1964 (for American coins), for buying of needed supplies should dollars completely die and not be accepted at the stores.

3. Gold coins for the larger amounts you wish to preserve and save, but not necessarily use during the depression. Or you could use them for larger purchases of items, like a car, house, etc.

This is good advice, but with one correction—have very few dollars on hand. The risk is too great to hold them. They may buy very little, or they may be discounted completely by the government and the people. If you are holding several thousand dollars this way, you could lose their value completely. If you place that purchasing power into silver coins (for the smaller, everyday purchases) instead of leaving large amounts in dollars, you are bound to come out on top.

You will use silver coins for grocery items, gas, small purchases, and transportation needs.

You will use gold for the larger savings and accumulations of wealth that you have secured over the years.

Both coins are equally important for differing reasons, as indicated. If prices fall as we have indicated, and you possess silver coins, you will be able to buy $50 worth of groceries (at today's prices) for only $5 to $10 dollars in the crash.

As I write this report, your silver quarter is already worth more than a dollar; if it rises further before the crash comes, imagine what silver will be worth when the crash actually hits! It will rise tremendously in value and purchasing power.

Why is silver so well-received, and why is it such a good store of value? The following points will enable you to understand this clearly.

1. Silver is a metal whose usefulness and rarity make it one of the two top metals in demand today. It is considered a precious metal for this reason.

2. Silver is the second most workable metal known to man. It easily adapts itself to the production requirements of every new application. This means that its economic base is continually and easily expanded.

3. Because of its beauty, silver's value was established so well that coins were made of it 4,000 years ago. Silver coins have consistently held their value and worth without fail from nation to nation, and from one political system to another.

4. Because of silver's whiteness and reflectivity, entire industries are built upon it. Certain industries must have silver, for nothing else known to man can take its place.

5. Many corporations and governments throughout the world have major research efforts underway to harness the energy of the sun, for ecological purposes and to meet the ever-rising need for more power and less reliance on foreign oil. Silver will be high on the list of essential ingredients to use the radiant energy of the sun. In this area alone, it is anticipated that the demand for silver could triple its annual consumption overnight, as research develops.

6. Each year the electrical and electronic industries use millions and millions of ounces of silver. Every computer, radio or TV station, jet airliner, submarine, rocket, spaceship, and surgical monitoring equipment, as well as an endless number of other items throughout the world, uses silver in its electrical and electronic systems. These industries' share of the world's consumption of silver increased 2 percent in just one year (1970-1971). Recent breakthroughs may increase consumption of silver in the next decade by 200 to 300 percent.

7. The entire photographic industry is based upon the light-sensitivity of silver. It is 100 times more efficient than the second most light-sensitive material. Millions of dollars have been spent looking for a silver substitute, but to no avail so far.

8. Silver is essential to the life and success of many industries; without it they would be crippled. This is a result of the natural properties found only in silver, which keeps it in high demand. These demands have created an economic base which expands daily.

9. Within the past decade, the U.S. government was forced to abandon silver in its coinage because the value to industry was so great that it rapidly exceeded the value placed on it in the coins. For example, by today's changing standards (it could be worth more right now), a pre-1964 silver quarter is worth over a dollar in silver content! That makes it worth 400 percent of its face value!

10. In 1971 the Silver Institute reported the expanding use of fine silver that numbered 22 recent developments. A technique for applying silver directly to stainless steel allows the strength of steel with the beauty of silver. The addition of only 1 percent of silver to the plates of lead-acid batteries doubles the life of the plates. This usage of silver opens the way to pollution-free cars. It is expected that during the decade of the 80's the manufacture of TV cassette recorder-players could use more than twice the silver than is now being produced annually!

11. As a bactericide, silver can be introduced into the water supply and controlled with an ion-sensitive electrode instrument, which will measure and monitor the silver content. It is odorless, tasteless, nontoxic, and inexpensive. Kodak is using and producing low-cost diffusion-transfer printing plates which use silver in the production of the printing image for the quick-copy reproduction field.

12. The technique of seeding certain types of clouds with silver-iodide particles to precipitate rainfall is proving to be profitable and is becoming more and more dependable in saving farmlands from crop loss due to lack of

rainfall.

13. Batteries used in portable appliances use silver electrodes and anhydrous silver-salt electrolytes.

14. Silver is also an outstanding catalyst in the production of antifreeze and various plastics.

15. Silver is irreplaceable and is essential in a multitude of applications that we have found for it currently and are discovering almost daily. As we become technically more sophisticated, silver becomes more and more irreplaceable.

16. For 100 years silver has been in an oversupply position, but now, due to ever-expanding uses of silver, the oversupply is gone. This could mean huge profits to silver holders as the price continues to rise to meet the demands.

17. At the end of World War II, the U.S. Government had 3 billion ounces of silver stockpiled. They had to use the silver to pay war debts to other nations who would not accept our paper currency at the time. That consumed over one-third of the silver in the U.S. stockpile. In the postwar years technology expanded the use of silver by industry, but supplies in the earth were rapidly running out, and mines were closing.

18. It has been over 45 years since a major discovery of silver has been found. So the chances of a major find now are remote indeed.

19. Geologists explain that silver is formed by what they call "epithermal depositions." This means that when the earth was being formed and molten masses began to cool, silver formed on the outer edge of the earth's

surface. This meant that most of the earth's silver (its richest and largest deposits) are almost on top of the ground.

20. 75 percent of today's silver that is produced from mining operations comes as the by-product of mining lead, zinc, or copper.

21. Though a vein of copper or lead may be very rich, the amount of silver in it diminishes the deeper the vein goes into the depths of the earth.

22. It is now estimated that, at the present rate of consumption of silver throughout the world, and at its present rate of production from the earth, we can expect the natural supply to drop very sharply within the next 10 years. It may dry up completely within the next 15 years.

23. At the present rate of silver production and consumption, the entire above-the-ground amount available to supply the deficit will not last another 2 years.

24. With the uses and demands for silver increasing constantly, and with no substitute found with the same qualities, the price of silver could explode in no time, and in fact is already going up rapidly, from the early days of $1.29 per ounce to today's price of $5.25 per ounce and rising.

25. It is true that an economic recession or depression would slow the industrial consumption of silver, **but not nearly as much as its production from the earth itself**. Thus, a depression would increase the deficit between supply and demand, making silver even more valuable. Also, in a depression, when paper money has lost its monetary value and its pur-

chasing power is gone, the need for silver in the mind of man will increase a million percent. Not many people are thinking this way today, but just let the dollar die overnight, and then see how alert and alive the mind of your neighbor will be to where he can get some silver! This will put silver in short supply, as everyone will want it. Those holding silver will enjoy its tremendously increased value.

26. Silver is in short supply, and the supply is getting smaller as industrial, military, and monetary needs arise. Silver is soon destined to become one of the **greatest wealth-makers of all times**.

27. Today a silver dollar sells for 4 paper dollars or more! Thus it still buys 8 to 10 loaves of bread, as it did back in 1940. The price of bread has not really gone up! It is just the value of paper money that has gone down! Interestingly enough, the true value of many products has stayed proportionate to the other true values of real purchasing power (gold and silver).

28. Silver has true wealth. It does not merely **represent** true wealth; it **is** true wealth. Therefore silver is inflation insurance, depression money, and excellent security for old age and for any period of life.

29. Any individual who intends to preserve his earnings and accumulated wealth to their maximum extent must take a look at the devaluation holding his wealth in dollars. The steady erosion of the dollar as paper money means the steady erosion of his wealth.

Silver does not diminish your wealth, or

erode your capital, as do paper holdings. Silver does not act in accordance with the current monetary systems of the world, which are not backed by gold or silver. It stands alone as a safe store of value on its own merit and quality. It also usually increases in value proportionate to the decrease in value of the paper-money systems. Those people who hold silver during a time of devaluation of currency due to "rapid-fire printing presses" strengthen their financial position at least to the exact ratio of the decrease of the monetary unit that is being devalued, and usually much more. If the dollar goes **down** in value 10 times, silver will go **up** in value 10 times. Which would you rather have—dollars or silver?

30. While the U.S. dollar went down constantly after demonetization of gold and the demonetization of silver from coins, the three nations holding to gold in Europe,—West Germany, Switzerland, and Holland—have had their currencies increased tremendously because they are backed by gold and silver holdings.

31. While the U.S. is selling its last ounce of gold on the auctions recently announced and engaged in, the central banks of Europe are buying it and are increasing their holdings up to 400 and 500 percent and more! The Russians are buying gold, China is on a gold-buying spree, and so are the Arabs, who are heavy in petro-dollars that lose their value every day.

Do you wonder if there really is a conspiracy to destroy the currency of this country when all around us so many other countries are so much better off than we? Are we really this stupid in government? Or is this planned, programmed, and on schedule?

32. Silver, like gold, holds its value abroad too (if you are planning on moving around from country to country in the coming crash). Silver is universally accepted, and will be even more so in the coming days.

33. In this nation, during and after the crash, if we have sold off our gold and silver supplies in a futile effort to shore up the dollar through patchwork economics, what will happen when **real** money is needed to rebuild the country after the depression? There must be the rebuilding of old enterprises and the building of new ones, thus creating new jobs, stores, factories, credit, development, and supplies for a growing and prosperous nation. If credit is gone because it is based on the dollar, and the money is almost totally devalued and despised by others and is continually distrusted, how are we going to rebuild? With what money? With what government reserve for just such an emergency?

Surely this has been thought out by the conspirators. They know, by enacting legislation to sell the gold and dump the silver on the markets, and then by **dumping stock and billions of dollars as earlier presented**, that they put the nation in an impossible position financially and economically.

With greenbacks devalued and distrusted, and the government hated by the people for allowing this to happen, and with no gold or silver reserves to buy help and development, we have only one recourse—**to join the movement toward utopia in Europe.**

They will have the gold; they will possess

the silver; they will have the new money system set up.

34. In 1929 the U.S. had extensive gold and silver holdings, but in this crash she will have little or none. This is a manipulated economic move toward certain economic suicide! We will govern ourselves to a limited local extent, but the brains of the leaders from Europe will determine our course. It could mean **the death of the sovereignty of the United States and the birth of the one-world government.**

You can at least be as independent as possible by owning silver!

Chapter

8

How to Survive the Coming Depression

In 1929, when the great crash came, it found many manipulators of finance safely out of dollars and into gold and silver. They moved just in time, for they knew what was happening or assumed it would happen. They were the safe ones; they moved out of paper money into hard money, that maintained itself through the crash and bought fortunes for them overnight!

The Newport Beach, California broker I mentioned earlier told us his father became a millionaire (at least once) by holding gold just before the crash developed and then buying up many pieces of real estate just for taxes!

It appears fairly certain that the depression will come. It is not really a question of **if** it comes; the question is, **when** will it arrive?

The depression is planned. It is going to be coordinated and orchestrated to a superlative degree with other conspiratorial plans, all leading to the deterioration of the will of the people of the United States and the death of the sovereignty of the United States, for all intents and purposes.

In the emergency situation already described, when the billions of dollars by overseas nations are dumped on Thursday, and then the stocks are dumped on Friday and the banks close on Monday in utter panic, pandemonium will break loose in this country and

Canada, and maybe some other countries which are also set up for the kill.

The net result in Washington will be utter confusion and many statements of self-justification with everyone blaming everyone else, especially one party blaming the other. As a result of such mass confusion and deterioration of control, in a short time it will become obvious to the American people—now struggling to eat and to find a place to live—that the government has the option of trying to go it alone and bring us out of the terrible dilemma, or else to join with forces that are far more viable, stable and secure—forces that guarantee a quick recovery for the United States by their wealth, ingenuity, and complete backing and support.

Many of these new-world leaders are Americans (along with their European and Oriental counterparts) as part of the new Trilateral Commission. They will come out smelling like a rose, looking as bewildered as the rest of us, but with altruistic humanitarianism dripping from every word they speak on behalf of the suffering American public.

Publicly they will share the grief of all, but privately they will be on top, financially holding gold, silver and utility stocks that can only rise as utilities rise in value as factories need coal, steel, and energy (oil) to get the nation back off its knees again.

They will offer the nation the option of struggling alone or taking their advice: "Give up some of the power of self-government in Washington and join the frugal, cautious world-planners who know the needs of America and who will reconstruct the country and government properly. After all, we all agree that it was terrible government spending that brought about this terrible and tragic depression anyway. We all know that it was government mismanagement, higher and higher taxes, and absurd use of the printing presses that produced the American crash.''

Knowing that the nation agrees, they will have an ace in their hand, and many of the American people will even fight for such a move, unpatriotic as it may seem to others.

Certain politicians will wholeheartedly agree. They know where their bread is buttered. Others will scream that it is the death knell of the United States. Still others will say, ''What alternative do we have? We have no gold or silver to rebuild with.''

Always before in a time of worldwide or American crisis, we have had gold to restore confidence in the treasury. Where is it going now? It is being sold at auctions to help the dollar as a patchwork Band-Aid to cover the ridiculous government printing of money for government exploitation.

This time it will be different entirely.

Many forecast that all of this will begin in 1980. Some think we have enough resiliency in the economy to bounce a while, till about 1983-85. But there are volatile problems that could affect the entire subject and precipitate the crash sooner than we think. I am speaking of bank failures due to defaulting on loans by third-world countries, or the Arab oil embargo, or the Arabs withdrawing their investments and savings in our banking institutions, or the uncertainties of the stock market and its vulnerability to a crash any day.

Any of these might trigger the blast-off, to say nothing of just world reaction to the dying dollar, in deciding to dump it any day now!

How can you survive the crash, whether it is here within 12 months or 5 years?

Several good books and many articles have been written on the subject during the last three years.

Let's discuss where you should be, and let's make a list of items that are most necessary for you to remember, to secure, and to have in your possession during the coming crash.

According to many writers, the last place you want to be is in the metropolitan cities, where violence, crime, food shortages, and general consumer confusion and bitterness may explode into social earthquakes. Civil unrest and disorder will be worst where the most people are living.

GET OUT OF TOWN AS QUICKLY AS POSSIBLE IF YOU LIVE IN A METROPOLITAN AREA.

Is it possible for you to find a retreat for yourself that meets most of the needs you'll have at that time? If so, then do what you can now to rent it, buy it, or build it, but **secure it** for the day of trouble ahead. It needs to be a place a long way from any metropolitan areas, preferably at least 200 miles—the farther the better.

Your retreat needs to be self-sustaining in utilities. What if power shortages come? There will be no electricity, oil, or gas for cooking or heating! What would you do? Think about it now. You must be in a position to have auxiliary means of heating, such as firewood or reserves of oil or gas. You must be able to use the firewood in a **wood stove** for cooking and heating. Time should be spent **now** preparing the wood and fuels in underground tanks for the day ahead. You will need enough for perhaps a 2-year supply! Better to have too much than too little.

In this mountain cabin or desert retreat or small farm that you will secure, keep in mind that your area of planted vegetables should not be visible from the road. Hide your garden on the other side of the hills. If you cannot be in a position to have a garden, make sure you start buying **now** and putting away in your retreat house or cabin such things as dehydrated foods or freeze-dried foods that have a shelf life of over 12 years and are easily stored in much less space than normal canned foods. Some of the water-canned foods are good too, and will last, but they take up much more space than dried foods.

You will need to think of not being able to shop, perhaps for months! Sit down and write a list of your needs, from flour to sugar, from salt and pepper to coffee, tea, and chocolate. List all the pots and pans and dishes you will require to feed your family, and don't forget dish soap, cleansers, scouring pads, scrapers, towels, deodorants, and a few phone books for bathroom tissue!

You'll almost have fun thinking about all the things you and your family will need as each family member makes a list, then all of you compare lists for variety and thoughtfulness. Then make your master list of things for survival. It may be a long list, but if you start now, you'll make it.

Saws, hatchets, axes, tools, rope, pails, barrels for rainwater, ladder, nails, screws, bolts, clothesline wire, and a thousand other useful items in a toolshed will be needed. A woodshed may also house a horse, or a snowmobile, or other auxiliary means of transportation. If you are going to live in the snow, remember that this requires certain types of boots and clothing, plus lots of firewood. If you have children, a sleigh or two and an old toboggan fills many a day.

Does all of this sound ridiculous to you? You would be surprised at how many hundreds of thousands of Americans have already secured their retreat with some living on it right now! Some of the very financial consultants quoted in this book live on and in their retreats this very minute! They have seen the crash coming, have sold their city houses and properties, and have moved out!

Living alone in the wilderness has its complications, but your forefathers accomplished it with much less than you will have, so you will survive it safely and comfortably if you act now.

Books will be needed for children's studies, pastime reading and entertainment. Battery-powered, transistorized radios or even television sets might be useful, depending on how close you are to stations and channels. But don't count on too much TV. Instead, think about **self**-entertainment. Most Americans without a TV set blaring go crazy with too much time on their hands.

The ideal location is in a moderate climate not requiring much heat or air conditioning, with your shelter secluded in the trees and hidden from too many prying eyes. If you build a place, put it where you can have visibility from every window, preferably with a clearing all the way around the house between you and the trees, so you will always be able to see who is coming or what is happening.

Stock your shelter with canned goods as indicated, and forget about having a lot of refrigeration if things get really bad. Plan on electricity working, and be hooked up to it if you can, but also consider your own generator and your own sources of power internally.

You must have an ample supply of water, either in your own drilled or dug well or in a freshwater lake or stream nearby. This is your big essential. You can always use dehydrated milk or cream, and if you check into it you will find a host of edible things that you can have on hand permanently without requiring refrigeration. Study carefully your plans for providing adequate food and water.

For those of us who can't move to the country or to the mountains or desert, what is required of us?

Perhaps you live in the city and feel you cannot get out. Perhaps you are too old to go, or are incapacitated, or have to stay there for medical attention. There are many reasons why millions of people will stay in the cities, but the biggest reason is money; many people can't afford the luxury of a private retreat in the Sierra mountains, or in the fiords of the Rockies, or in northern Canada's wilds, that are so beautiful and so full of rivers to fish. (Keep in mind—you could live off of a river for a long time!)

If you stay in the city, make sure you have as safe a place as possible, with a bolt lock on your door and secure window locks. Buy dehydrated food and store it under your bed, in the closet, in the pantry, and anywhere else that you can safely store food to last a year or more.

Supplement this food with normal, water-canned preserved food. The stores are still full of it, but don't wait too long.

Make your list, and spend some money on it each week or each month, building up your supply constantly. Don't wait for a "more convenient time" to do it. Do it now! Bottled water can be bought and stored in case your water supply is temporarily cut off. I do not foresee this happening for long.

But what if the electricity went off? You would not have air conditioning, although you can live without this. You also might not have heat, since many heating systems have electrical controls. I know of people who have bought a small wood-burning stove for their kitchen. Imagine an old-fashioned "jacket heater" with pipes going out the window and you pouring in the wood to keep the kitchen and maybe another room or two warm! Get yourself a sleeping bag too. No harm in sleeping by the fireplace or heater if necessary—it could be downright romantic!

You can always cook something on that "jacket heater" too. You can heat your coffee water and tea water and even take an old-fashioned "kitchen sponge bath"!

One of the fondest and loveliest memories of my life is when as a boy of 12 I lived on a farm with my sister and her husband while my mother was recuperating in the hospital from an illness. We did not have electricity or indoor running water or bathroom facilities. We had an outdoor well, an outdoor cutting spot for cutting firewood, and an outdoor path and backhouse that would freeze your buttocks and make you shiver just to think of it now, especially when it was 40 below zero at night, and you had an emergency call and just had to go!

I had a "baseball bedroom" upstairs, unheated. It had a "pitcher on the dresser and a catcher underneath the bed." There were plenty of blankets, candles, and coal-oil lanterns, and a battery radio that delighted me as a child.

Now you can buy chemical toilets for your cabin that have chemicals for the disintegration of solids and destruction of all odors, for those of you moving to the hills.

Don't forget to get triplicate fulfillments of your prescriptions now, in glasses, medicines, and special personal needs requiring prescriptions. Who knows how close you will be to a functioning chemist, pharmacist, druggist, doctor, nurse, or dentist then? Many stores and offices will close. Get as much done **now** in dental work and personal betterment that you possibly can. We may be roughing it ahead.

Not all services are going to be stopped for city dwellers, but they may be interrupted from time to time. Get those candles and keep them accessible. When the power goes off now, we have ours handy. A coal-oil or kerosene or camping stove can be a help as well. (Never burn charcoal in your house or apartment.

It consumes too much air, and with windows closed it is often fatal.)

Think about your clothing needs. Don't worry about being stylish, but just comfortable. The weather you will live in will determine what you need.

In addition to furnishing your apartment or home or cabin properly with all the above items and the additional ones you will think of, remember to have a gun for self-protection. There is nothing like a deterrent if someone unsavory knocks on the door. You may want more than one weapon. A good shotgun with lots of ammunition nearby and a small loaded handgun make good precautions against snoopers, thieves, and criminals in general.

The best place to live, if you can afford the time to find it, and can afford to live there, is a small, self-sustaining town of about 10,000 people. They have their own doctors, small hospital, stores, banks, and a "general feeling of knowing everybody in town." Friendliness is most important. This town could support itself with food grown by the local farmers and everyone who has his own garden. In this type of town, you will find people who will share with you readily and kindly and love doing it!

Better than this, in this small town you can get into a good friendly church, where people tend to love one another and be friendly, making friends of God's children and together preparing for the days of trouble ahead.

Two or three families might move in together into an adequate mountain home or cabin. Each of the men might be proficient in some way, perhaps differing from one another in talent. A Red Cross course in first aid has often been recommended to me by my wife. She wants to take one this winter to be better prepared to take care of her family this way. A good idea!

Stay out of areas and towns that could have racial explosions. The coming social disorder resulting from the currency crash, as Johnny Johnson said, could very well produce terrible social unrest, so that racial tensions could flare. Check out where you are going for this potential first. Also, stay away from small towns that have only one or two heavy industries or large plants where most of the people are employed. If industry fails and manufacturing falls off, as we know it will, these people will not be self-sustaining. Trouble could develop within the town by those without funds and without a garden or farm, as they disturb those people who are self-sustaining.

There are many small towns around the country that produce their own food supply of grains, cattle, truck crops, and general food goods that everyone needs. They are not dependent on trucking and trains to bring in their survival foods. These towns usually also have plenty of their own wells, and usually a good police force and fire department.

Some of us would really love getting "back to the country." Smell that fresh, unpolluted air; breathe in that sweetness flowing from the fields; stick your feet in the country stream and forget the sounds of freeway traffic; gone are the days of getting all nervous and impatient waiting for the long line of cars to move another 10 feet!

Getting back to family living as it once was will be beautiful: Walks on the country roads; enjoying nature; eating some new foods freshly picked or dug from the soil. (Pardon me while I dream a while! But why don't you dream too?)

Now to the big subject—how to survive **financially** (as well as socially and physically, as we have just discussed). How can you survive financially and even come out on top financially?

One of at least three things will happen to you. You could be prepared to an extent and survive fairly well, or else you could fail to prepare and suffer terribly, or else, you could prepare well, survive well, and make a fortune in the coming crash.

Which of these will happen to you depends on how willing you are to act now. Are you willing to move your assets **now** into secure assets, and take the losses this move will cost you at this present time?

For example, are you prepared to go to your savings and loan and/or bank and draw your money out of your savings accounts and lose some interest on it? You may be fortunate and find that it is interest time, and therefore not lose as much as you had anticipated. But don't count on it. It never seems to be "the right time" to draw money out of the institutions. This will cost you some lost interest.

Also, are you prepared for the inconvenience of having to sell your home and all that this entails? Are you ready to move to a rented place rather than own? This makes some people very uncomfortable psychologically. They feel they must "own." But if you can wait until after the crash, you **will** own again and at a much lower rate of payment or purchase price than now.

Sell out your stocks and bonds, taking your present losses or gains; liquidate all your assets. Plan on buying gold coins, and U.S. silver coins minted up to and including 1964.

Divide your savings money (money you do not need right now) into half gold and half silver. If this is a lot of money, then divide it two-thirds into gold and one-third into bags of silver. Remember, silver buys the groceries, and gold is for bigger purchases and for larger amounts to be saved from the crash.

How much greenback currency you keep should also be decided, because you do not want to use your gold and silver savings for living expenses now. You have to keep some amounts of dollars in your account to write utility checks, etc. But keep it fluid with not too much in the bank at any time. Keep putting your money into the bank and writing it out. Deal in dollars until it is no longer wise, prudent, and practical to do so. Continue to buy coins as well.

Do not tell a soul about your gold and silver holdings. That will be hard for some people who like to brag and talk a lot. But a slip of the lip could cause you great worry and trouble later on. People will remember that you said you had gold, silver, dehydrated food, bottled water, a retreat, a place of refuge in the time of storm. Keep quiet! This is most essential. You do not have to tell all to your children, either. Do not allow them to be put into the position of "blowing the family dream for survival." We are talking about important things.

By purchasing South African Krugerrand gold coins, or Austrian Coronas, etc., you are buying safety, certainty, and assured insurance for yourself and family now. You are buying peace of mind for the present, and you are securing your savings for the future with some good living.

Perhaps you are very busy in business with others or for yourself, and/or you are very gainfully employed. You do not want to move now. You cannot get out right away.

Then stay in business if you want to take the risk of losing much of what you have in it when the crash comes. You may be right to stay there now. What you would lose by staying in now may be more than offset by your present earnings till the crash comes. If by selling out your business now you can make it in the small town or retreat, then do so. But perhaps you can have the best of both worlds by looking around and making the physical plans to retreat when it all happens, yet remaining in business as long as you see it safe to do so.

If it takes selling your home now to get your money out of it, to put into gold and silver, then do it. Sell while real estate is high in price. Do not wait until calamity strikes and no one will have the money to buy anything.

If you had invested only $5,000 in gold 6 years ago, you would have made over 600 percent on your investment, which would be at approximately $31,000!

Had you invested $10,000 in gold then, you would have $62,000 today!

Had you invested in silver at the rate of $5,000, you would have over $20,000 today! It's not that real estate has not increased in value, or that your business may not have increased in value. But will they both continue to rise as the depression comes? No. But gold and silver will!

The question is often asked of me in my seminars, "Where do we safely store our gold or silver?" You could keep it in a safe deposit box in the bank, but if the banks fold, or close for any reason, you are without it. In some areas there are safety-deposit-box companies that are not banks, but are independent companies where you can secure a guarded safety deposit box for valuables.

My best advice is, keep your gold and silver at home, safely stored in a safe cemented into the floor, and pray! Or else select a spot in the wall or floor where only you will know how to get at it, and keep your gold and silver there.

Properly stored in a safe, your valuables will be safe from destruction in a fire, earthquake, etc. Your big problem is thieves. Get some good advice from the store selling you the safe, and get an alarm system that is hooked up to the local police-station and also has a loud-sounding alarm. There are some very sophisticated alarm systems which are worth their weight in gold!

In addition to the foregoing ideas on survival and making a fortune for yourself in the coming depression, this book would not be complete without my philosophy on the greatest insurance of all for the coming crash.

Most of this material has been presented independent of religious or Biblical prophetic thoughts, but now let me assure you that your greatest insurance for the days ahead lie with God almighty and His power to protect you, guide you, and sustain you whether you have possessions or whether you have nothing of a material sense with which to be helped.

God loves you, and He especially wants to take care of you if you have accepted His Son Jesus Christ as your personal Savior and Lord, as indicated in John 3:16-17.

The 23rd Psalm is yours; you will be able to say during the crash:

"The Lord is my Shepherd; I shall not want. He maketh me to lie down in green pastures; He leadeth me beside the still waters. He restoreth my soul; He leadeth me in the paths of righteousness for His name's sake. Yea, though I walk through the valley of the shadow of death, I will fear no evil for Thou art with me; Thy rod and Thy staff, they comfort me. Thou preparest a table before me in the presence of mine enemies; Thou anointest my head with oil; my cup runneth over. Surely goodness and mercy shall follow me all the days of my life, and I will dwell in the house of the Lord forever."

When you have nothing material, you still have Him. If you have no gold or silver today with which to help yourself, you still have Him. He works miracles, and He will take care of you as His own. He is greater than all the gold and silver in the world!

Keep your faith in God. Keep reading His Word daily. In it you have guidance and strength for any task and for whatever comes your way.

Keep praying daily. God answers prayers of mine constantly, and for millions of other people who put their trust in Him. Pray positively, never begging God negatively, for he is the One who has promised to take care of you. Read Psalms 90 and 91 when all hell breaks loose around you!

Notes